Self-Sufficient Housing

Housing

1st Advanced Architecture Contest

The Competition

Organize

Collaborate

MINISTERIO DE VIVIENDA

Generalitat de Catalunya
Departament de Medi Ambient
i Habitatge
Direcció General d'Habitatge

fundación caja de arquitectos

Fundació UPC

The Advanced Architecture Contest is a new way to promote knowledge using the Internet as an open, global space for research. The Institute for Advanced Architecture of Catalonia has offered the international architectural community a subject for reflection (the self-sufficient house) that is applicable from the entire world to the entire world. The result will serve as the basis for a research exercise to be conducted in greater depth at the IaaC campus in Barcelona.

Thus, we proposes the initiation of a biannual process that will stimulate social, technical and cultural progress, as well as promote the advancement of architecture.

Francesc Fernandez i Joval President of IaaC

Legend

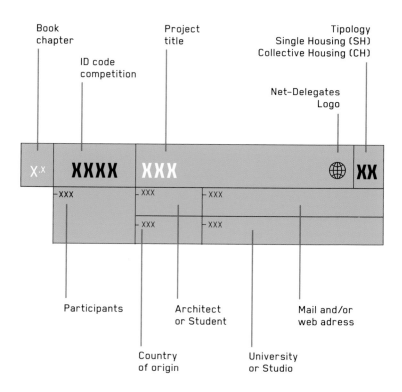

Book chapter

ID code competition

Project title

Tipology
Single Housing (SH)
Collective Housing (CH)

Net-Delegates Logo

X.x

XXXX

XXX

⊕

XX

XXX

XXX

XXX

XXX

XXX

Participants

Architect or Student

Mail and/or web adress

Country of origin

University or Studio

Contents

Vicente Guallart
Director of IaaC

Self-sufficient habitat

In the early 20th century, the concept of "dwelling" was defined as a "machine for living," a reference to a new way of understanding the construction of inhabitable spaces that characterized the Machine Age. Today, a century later, we face the challenge of constructing a sustainable or even self-sufficient dwelling, now a living organism that interacts with its environment, exchanging resources, and which functions as an entirely self-sufficient entity, like a tree in a field. The aim of advanced architecture is not to produce a dwelling that is simply the product of economics. On the contrary, advanced architecture aspires to create the conditions of individual inhabitation, one that meet day-to-day needs, on different scales and at different times. The project of human inhabitation is resolved in a local environment, on the scale of the district, the building or the individual limits of a dwelling. A self-sufficient dwelling is one that is connected to this local system and knows how to respond to the social, cultural, technical and economic conditions of its surroundings. It will also be able to administer its place in the global information network, one comprised of similar organisms, all sharing resources and information, engaged in remote interaction.

In the day-to-day of Western countries, we are astonished to see how the price of urban housing is rising without an objective increase in value. We must insist that these dwellings adapt their specific qualities to their market price. The objective increase in the value of a space is directly linked to a potential savings in long-term maintenance and running costs. As such, we need to call for the design and construction of buildings that generate 100% of the energy they consume, recycle all the water they use (by means of various processes) and locally generated waste (which may be capable of generating new a materiality).

In the 20th century, high-level availability and energy consumption were international paradigms for development; in the 21st-century, the new paradigm is one of saving and the intelligent use of available resources at an interconnected local level.

Architecture now faces a new responsibility of having to respond to these needs. Districts, buildings and dwellings should be able to incorporate new elements such as sensors, accumulators or transformers of synergies that would replace insulating skins that isolate dwellings from the changing climate of their surroundings.

We must ask more of architecture. We architects should be required to design inhabitable organisms that are capable of developing functions and integrating the processes of the natural world that formerly took place at a distance in other points of a surrounding territory. Subcontracting energy creation in a distant place seems to be a thing of the past, like dependency on remote computation for data processing.

Hence, the challenge is to think about the design of buildings and dwellings in this new situation and to develop building design and construction in an integrated fashion, rather than continue with the current trend of simply superimposing catalogued technological solutions onto buildings and purely formal considerations. Research into the development of materials requires the updating of the materiality of buildings and the improvement of centuries-old construction techniques, which are very closely based on the transformation of locally available materials. It is now time for the interaction between disciplines and technologies with a view toward producing solutions that embrace different fields of research.

The 1st Advanced Architecture Contest was organized as a strategy to stimulate research into new ways of understanding the phenomenon of inhabitation. A whole range of practicing architects and students took a local approach to their designs, presenting very different attitudes and ideas about their understanding of "self-sufficiency." This book presents a selection of these proposals and represents the first step in what will be a long-lasting body of research that seeks to stimulate the development of an architecture, a way of building and a more intelligent form of inhabitation.

1 .2

Willy Müller
Development
Director IaaC

Common sense

The debate about the self-sufficiency of advanced societies is a continuation of the historical process of reflection regarding the survival needs that are shared by all societies. An essential part of this process is the debate about the crisis of the energy model, one that (as I see it) involves extremely direct consequences for issues that have been relevant for centuries, such as the model of coexistence in a particular territory and its respective scales: cities, buildings, homes, etc.

This is a crisis that starts with energy but ends with problems of the scale of the consumer model, with the models of dependency acquired by these scales and new values of sustainability. How can we apply ourselves to the idea of self-sufficiency without lapsing into romantic nihilism (predictions of varying degrees of doom and gloom) or disproportionate optimism (marked by nearly a century's worth of literature, speculation and experimentation)?

Regarding this issue, many pages have been written by members of our discipline such as Archigram (great theorists with prolific imaginations who were sterile in terms of action) or conversely, the empiric passion of individuals such as Buckminster Fuller, who devoted much of his energy to energy and offered some very advanced proposals on the subject of self-sufficiency, timelessness, sustainability and independence.

Once again we have to ask questions, in the Socratic tradition that we have always

encouraged at Metapolis and the IaaC. However, we should change the manner in which
we understand the answers to our questions:
if we ask the Planet, we must be prepared to
receive the Planet's answers, which may lay
outside our habitual scales of understanding.
Does the concept of self-sufficiency jeopar-
dize the idea of the city that we have designed,
built and disfigured for centuries?
Alternatively, is the idea of sustainability
so subtle and delicate that it is possible to
be absolutely self-sufficient and completely
unsustainable? Would it be fair to say that the
impermanence of our models of coexistence
renders any non-dependent system of sufficiency completely inefficient?

Can we establish a formulaic system of variables to define the correct strategy for sufficiency or sustainability for a given place?
We must ask ourselves these questions.
In the face of this crisis, we must delve into common sense, particularly the commonest of these senses, consulting, comparing and contrasting different viewpoints from various places on our planet, understanding that the objective of globalism is to draw us together, a movement away from a singular way of seeing. Beyond thinking globally and acting locally, our goal should be to obtain a planet that thinks and acts globally.
What does the future hold for our small local histories?

WILL WE UNDERST

OF SELF-S

IN TERMS OF S

AND THE CONCEPT

UFFICIENCY

STAINABILITY?

WILL WE CREATE
PROJECTS FOR T
OF SELF-SUFF

ROPERLY SCALED

E DEVELOPMENT

CIENT MODELS?

WILL WE BE AB

TOTALLY DEPEN

OF SELF-SI

E TO REVERSE
NT PROCESSES
FFICIENCY?

ARE WE MAKI
TEMPORARY SE
OR OF PERMANENT

G MODELS OF

F-SUFFICIENCY

ELF-INSUFFICIENCY?

Lucas Cappelli
Director Advanced
Architecture Contest

Advanced knowledge

With the Internet, a horizontal technology that lays the foundations of information and communicating, we are dealing with a society that has the autonomous capacity for cultural creation marked by an increasing dissolution of pre-existing systems of bureaucratic control. This "flat technology," one free of specialization, without barriers of assimilation, offers new mechanisms that enable the absorption of information, which serve as a means of reaching solutions that become the base for the generation of new knowledge.

While traditional forms of knowledge production address and solve problems in a context governed by the interests of a specific community and is disciplinary, (both homogeneous and hierarchical) this new form develops in a context of application: it is transdisciplinary, heterogeneous, flexible, transitory, socially responsible and reflective.

This is the birth of a new form of knowledge production that includes a larger body of practitioners, ephemeral but linked in time, heterogeneous but interconnected, all working on a specific, delimited issue.

The scope of this issue also presumes the application of a transdisciplinary approach, since the resolution of these difficulties reaches beyond the individual discipline that constitutes them, placing discoveries beyond the confines of a single specific order and removing the need for a validating point of reference.

This new proceeding also assumes the presence of new mechanisms of diffusion.

The greater number of actors involved, with very different backgrounds of discipline and regional origins, greatly increases subsequent diffusion and, as a result, the production of new knowledge multiplies exponentially as it advances towards new applications and uses. The Advanced Architecture Contest proposes the verification of these proposals applied to a practical development of new, self-sufficient architectonic symbols; proposals that consider all of the confines of our planet and demonstrate that the exponential reprecussions and impact of the employment of this medium will provoking the reflection of a subject that should stop being definitively postponed. This subject of "sustainable destruction" represents the persistent abuse of our environment. Our goal is the implantation of a new, self-respecting human consciousness.

The background to this concern, which recognises how new knowledge production takes place, is the desire to formulate relevant questions addressing a hypothetical international strategy that will direct the way we use information towards the design of less self-destructive, more self-sufficient constructions.

All the projects presented here implicitly address this issue.

Canada 10
Mexico 38
USA 80

NA 128

Cuba 2
Dominican Republic 2
British West Indies 1
El Salvador 1

CA 6

Argentina 26
Bolivia 2
Brazil 5
Chile 20
Colombia 9
Peru 9
Uruguay 6
Venezuela 6

SA 87

Austria 6
Belarus 1
Belgium 1
Bosnia 1
Croatia 3
Denmark 2
France 31
Germany 17
Greece 11
Hungary 1
Italy 41
Lithuania 1
Netherlands 7
Norway 1
Poland 7
Portugal 12
Rumania 4
Russia 5
Serbia & Montenegro
Slovakia 2
Spain 25
Sweden 3
Turkey 5
UK 12

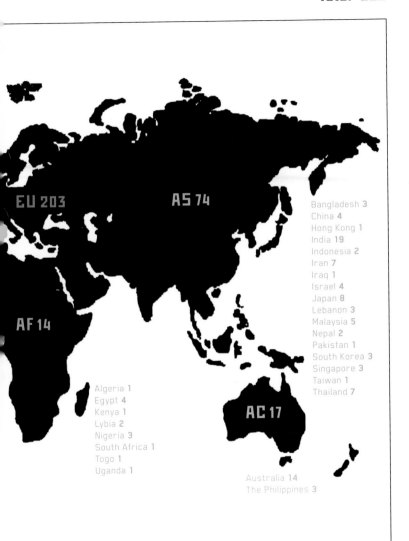

EU 203

AS 74

AF 14

AC 17

Bangladesh 3
China 4
Hong Kong 1
India 19
Indonesia 2
Iran 7
Iraq 1
Israel 4
Japan 8
Lebanon 3
Malaysia 5
Nepal 2
Pakistan 1
South Korea 3
Singapore 3
Taiwan 1
Thailand 7

Algeria 1
Egypt 4
Kenya 1
Lybia 2
Nigeria 3
South Africa 1
Togo 1
Uganda 1

Australia 14
The Philippines 3

1ˢᵗ Advanced Architecture Contest

Vicente Guallart, Director IaaC
Willy Müller, Development Director Iaac
Manuel Gausa, Actar Arquitectura (Barcelona)
Lucas Cappelli, Director Advanced Architecture Contest
Marta Malé-Alemany, Director Digital Tectonics IaaC
Luis Falcón, Director HyperEurope IaaC
José Luis Echevarría, Faculty IaaC
Jordi Mansilla, Faculty IaaC
Marta Cervelló, Architect, Fundación Caja Arquitectos
Felipe Pich-Aguilera, Architect (Barcelona)
François Roche, Architect, R&Sie Architects (Paris)
Jacob van Rijs, Architect, MVRDV (Rotterdam)
Aaron Betsky, Director, NAI (Rotterdam)
J.M. Lin, The Observer Design Group (Taipei)
Kim, Young Joon YO$_2$, Architects (Seoul)
Julio Gaeta, Architect, *El Arqa* magazine
José Miguel Iribas, Sociologist
Ignacio Jiménez de la Iglesia, Real estate strategist
Ramon Prat, Graphic Designer, Actar
Artur Serra, Antropologist, UPC
Salvador Rueda, Agencia d'Ecologia Urbana de Barcelona

The evaluation of the different projects by the international jury of the 1st Advanced Architecture Contest revealed a great level of diversity in the approaches to the concept of "Self-Sufficient Housing" and an excellent level of work. The jury awarded the following prizes:

1st prize in the category of Collective Housing:

Daniel Ibañez Moreno, Rodrigo Rubio Cuadrado, Alberto Alvarez Agea. ID Code: 83a3c.

The jury considers the the idea of negotiating and self-adjusting different sustainability programs within a building, as well as between different buildings, to be an inventive and interesting solution. That the proposal takes into account a multiplicity of self-imposed, as well as external, conditions also contributed to the sophistication and complexity of the final design.

1ˢᵗ prize in the category of Single Housing:

Gaetan Kohler. ID Code: 7e6cc.

The radical suggestion of exploiting local specificity makes this proposal interesting from a technical point of view. Moreover, this proposal was one among a small number of other entries that outlined a comprehensive and well schematised self-sufficiency agenda that was tied to local agricultural production. Jury members respoded positively to the way in which the final design relates to the existing landscape.

2ⁿᵈ prize: Nicolas Buckley, Kenny Orellana, Carlos Arguedas. ID Code: a41ea.

The interest of this proposal lies in its realistic approach towards sustainability, taking maximum advantage of lo-tech solutions in a context in where hi-tech solutions prove to be impossible. Two aspects make this proposal quite remarkable: First, the design arguments relate to the outerlying context, tying the proposal to large-scale economic and social agendas. Second, this proposal pursues an updated version of twentieth century housing remediation tactics.

3rd prize: Yukio Minobe. ID Code: e82db.
The proposal's main point of interest is the reformulation of the 2D "green roof" into a 3D surface. This tactic not only multiplies known effects, but also acts as a visual lure, attracting attention and transforming the skyline, a conspicuous reminder within the city.

IaaC Net_delegates

The jury would also like to acknowledge all the projects and architects, from all over the world, who presented diverse applications of self-sufficiency in a global scale, and grant these individuals the title of Iaac "Net-Delegates."

01d27	Austria – Eva M Silberschneider
02396	Libya – Muftah Abudajaja
02a84	Venezuela – Julio Ferrer Piñeiro, Maria Graciela Soto Fuenmayor
053e2	Italy – Olindo Merone, Edoardo Boi, Emanuele Pibiri
18f73	Lithuania – Lukas Narutis
229d4	India – Kalpesh Ramesh Solanki
22f8d	Belgium – Lode Vranken, Kitty Strybol, Jan Vermeylen
27aa5	China – Rujun Xie, Maoamo
288ad	Chile – Pablo Muñoz Bahamonde, Oscar Terrazas
2c35a	South Korea – Sung-yong Park
2fc6a	Thailand – Nutthawut Piriyaprakob
339b3	Greece – Juliet Zindrou, Xanthopoulos Pavlos, Blazetti Ezio
33a88	Sweden – Louise Jalilian, Petra Thedin, Koen Kragting
3f6d8	Iran – Mohamad Khabazi, Sara Norouzi, Keivan Saberi
3fa1f	France – Damien Mikolajczyk
527cd	Mexico – Ricardo Arandia, Alessandro Uras, Maria Ludovica Tramontin, Kristine
53265	Egypt – Sarah Eldefrawy
5bad8	Argentina – Lucas Martin Ruarte, Fabiana Agusto, Matteo Ferrari, Anna Malaguti, Francesco Tosi, Alberto Verde
60033	USA – Adelaide Dawn
65190	Bangladesh – Asaduzzaman Rassel

6ceca	Singapore – Joseph Ee Man Lim
6ecb7	UK – Roderick Tong, Lawrence Wong, Bianca Cheung
6fc40	Romania – Emil Ivanescu
6fe96	Croatia – Bruno Vodan Juricic
74e33	Cuba – Jorge Ramos
7f314	Canada – Eitaro Hirota, Sengsack Tsoi, Keith Ng, Tomoyuki Shimizu, Tsukasa Takenaka, Aya Okabe
8505d	Australia – Samuel Tan
8b8db	Serbia &Montenegro – Predrag Djermanovic, Tatic Nina
9b04e	Denmark – Kent Pedersen, Mathilde Petri, Marie Preisler Berthelin
9b179	Japan – Hideyuki Natsume, Sosuke Ito
a1204	Netherlands – Rop Van Loenhout, Rickerd Van Der Plas, Dennis Moet, Ludo Boeije
a127e	Malaysia – Mohd Redza Abdul Rahman, Mohd Daniel Iman Bin Mohd Delan, Ahmad Farihan Bin Sudirman
a53c7	Nigeria – Fareh Garba, Austin Seid
ac2fa	Russia – Simon Rastorguev, Alexei Magai
b0eed	Lebanon – Daniel Elias Georges
b5531	Nepal – Rabindra Adhikari
b5764	Brazil – Carolina Galeazzi, Leticia Teixeira Rodrigues, Gustavo Jaquet Ribeiro
b74ef	Colombia – Natalia Triana, Juan Carlos Bohorquez
b8fbd	Israel – Erez Amitay, Fioraso Francesca
bbd40	Uruguay – Esteban Varela Fernandez, Martin Delgado, Nicolás Barriola
bc2ff	Poland – Szymon Banka
cb86c	Spain – Paul Galindo Pastre, Ophélie Herranz Lespagnol
e8130	Portugal – Filipa Valente, Jorg Majer
efaf5	Germany – Tom Forster, Nadine Lachmund, Christian Raschke, Marko Schneider
f33a2	Taiwan – Jeong-der Ho, Deland Wai-man Leong

Leonardo Novelo
Architect

The sustainable house. Taxonomy

Throughout the world the building of contemporary housing represents a drastic environmental impact. In reponse to this situation, the Institute for Advanced Architecture of Catalonia has organized the 1st Advanced Architecture Contest, "Self-Sufficient Housing,"aimed at self-sustainable housing design.

A variety of positions and multiple conceptions regarding self-sufficient housing have been introduced through this competition.

All entries can be considered as a method of highly efficient intervention that integrates and unifies. Consequently, the various alternatives received in this competition show how the image and production of the self-sustainability have been considered, in mulitiplicity, throughout the entire world. There is no single and unique principle.

The sum of these projects yield an open taxonomy of interconnections.

The ordering of this form generated subsequent groupings: Bio and Bugs, Blow and Form, Collective, Modulated and Cost, Position and Site, Territorial and Community, Theory and Wrapped.

And in any case, without considering the classification, the self-sufficient house becomes immersed in pre-established cycles and avoids negative impacts while achieving a harmonic relationship with its surroundings.

Bio and Bugs

2.1	0aa06	Accomodation	
2.2	2c514	House in the breakwater	
2.3	22c53	Hydro Shell	
2.4	54510	Re-thinking Lascaux	
2.5	cc23c	CommandPOD	
2.6	f4a9b	The Carapace Project	
2.7	1f437	ALG.AE	
2.8	7e6cc	MicroCosm-House	1st Prize Single Housing
2.9	527cd	Actus	
2.10	f9008	Boomerang House	
2.11	a53c7	Above/Below Ground	

In its condition as such, the self-sufficient dwelling is configured and behaves in similar fashion to a living organism, as one element more in the natural process of the environment in which it participates. Once conceived and throughout the various phases of development, it will evolve according to processes of metamorphosis, adaptation and transformation in keeping with the laws that govern its surroundings. The Bio and Bug harmoniously adopts the characteristic codes of interrelation of the living organisms that inhabit the environment in which it is set, seeking to create the minimum impact in the process. Almost like an insect, sometimes nomadic, sometimes sedentary, it partakes in the mutual exchange of energy with the landscape. It does so without exception, not as a simple imitation of nature and the environment, but as an active element collaborating within a system. In this way, rather than being a foreign body, the bug integrates and becomes another element in the inherent cycles of the place. To this end, it uses only the necessary resources, attending to energy efficiency and the correct management of the waste matter produced for reinsertion into the local system.

This taxonomy includes the alternative of the Plug-in cell and the complete Biotope system, which was awarded first prize in the Self-Sufficient Single Housing Contest. The Plug-in cell, a cellular entity that successively returns to a higher urban organism, like a parasite to original buildings, favouring society's increasingly frequent nomadism, is absorbed into pre-existing structures and is therefore added to the external networks of communication and services, delegating to the host city the total administration of its waste. The Biotope system, conversely, forceful and exemplary in its approach, perceptive in its solution and therefore judicious and plausible as an alternative, behaves like an organism that is constructed basically of fabrics, fibres, straw and bamboo, which works its way into the topographic crop system (rice plantations) of the place and ably administers its resources with a full agenda of self-sufficiency that is in tune with the existing landscape, leaving it unchanged. Biotope also guarantees a significant social impression, since it is initially available to the peasant population of China. Its potential impact is, however, easily extensible to places with similar conditions, such as much of southern Asia, leaving its logic open to successive applications.

0aa06 — Accommodation

SH

Elodie Nourrigat Jacques Brion Gaetan Morales	Architect	www.nbarchi.com elodie@nbarchi.com
	EU_France	N+B architects

The city is full of excess energy and services, man's living requirements are today easily satisfied, man need only a place to sleep, to have a wash, to work, and to communicate. The place he lives in, is not the house, it's the city. Plug-in cell is a new kind of urban life estyle. It transplanted it to existing buildings and squatted excess energy using the existing networks visible in the streets. Plug-in cell is a self-sufficient house, due to the fact that it doesn't use new clean energy, but only existing network, recycling water, electricity excess, and filtering CO_2. Plug-in cell is a network hacker.

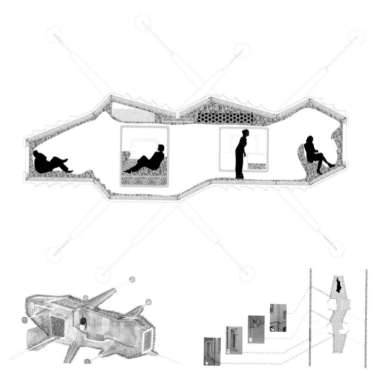

2cS14 · House in the breakwater · CH

- Pablo Twose
- Pancorbo Serna
- Maria Twose
  Perez de Rada
- Alberto Twose Valls

- Student

- ptwose@hotmail.com

- EU_Spain

- ETSAV

The project proposes a collective housing structure at the breakwater, humanizing a clearly artificial environment necessary to any harbouru town. The breakwater is a constant receiver of water, light and air. Out of these parameters we try to achieve the maximum natural efficiency. The shape of the breakwater compels us to distribute houses lengthwise and the houses work as a section which captures natural resources.

Use of natural resources: **WATER** Still solar (evaporation-condensation cycle); **LIGHT** Lighting, radiation, green house effect, and electricity (photovoltaic); **AIR** Bernoulli Effect, air conditioning, airiness and electricity (eolic).

The coast has prevailing winds from the sea to the ground: the marine breezes. The project responds to these breezes by means of a section similar to the shape of a wing of a plane, in order to create an air flow as described in the Bernoulli theorem. The marine breeze generates a vacuum on the upper part of the section thanks to the shape of the wing which sucks the air from the inner part of the building.

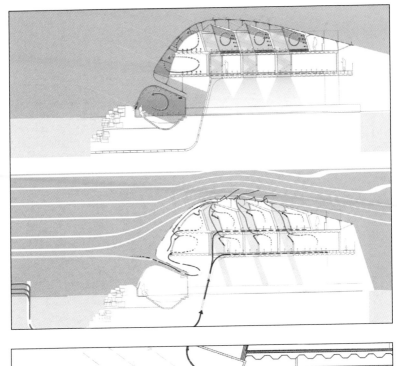

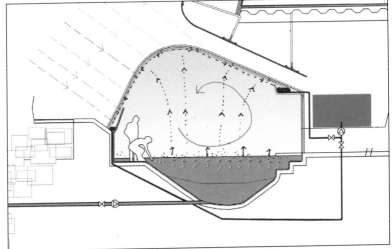

22c53 Hydro Shell SH

Styliani Daouti	Architect	sdaouti@gmail.com
	EU_Greece	Ecole d'Architecture de Paris-Belleville

Adaptation of a family house in the rapidly expanding Athenian coast:
HYDRO An open pool occupies the centre of the house, where sea and rain water is collected creating a natural cooling effect. The water is filtered and distributed through gravity to the lower part of the house where it becomes potable through a desalinating system. Electric energy is generated by the movement of water through a series of small turbines located below the house. **SHELL** The organism is sheltered by light recycled steel arcs, which are easily brought to site and are put together around a central structural ring. The structure is covered by a high resistance textile membrane and operable glass parts: Open during the summer for air circulation and closed during the winter for a green house effect. Solar panels cover partially the south part of the structure and produce additional electric energy. The house appears as an amphibious, independent organism almost like a shell full of water discovered on the shore.

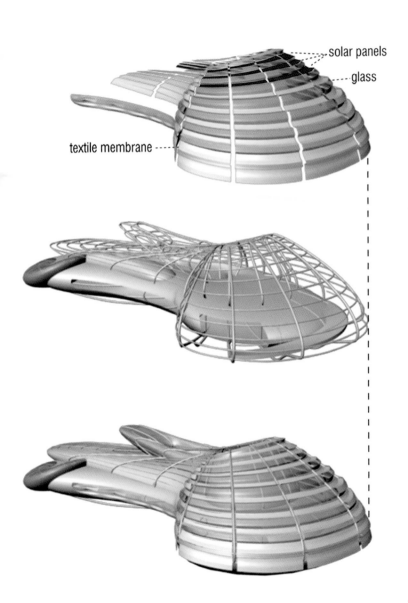

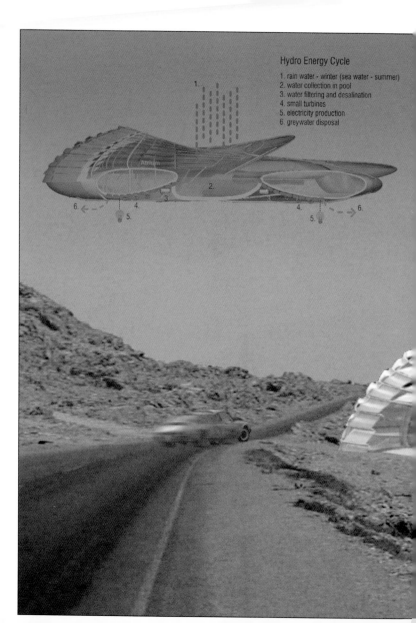

Hydro Energy Cycle

1. rain water - winter (sea water - summer)
2. water collection in pool
3. water filtering and desalination
4. small turbines
5. electricity production
6. greywater disposal

54510 Re-thinking Lascaux | CH

- Christoph Opperer
- Jörg Hugo
- Jens Mehlan

| - Architect | - off ice@moh-architecture.com |
| - EU_Austria | - moh | architecture |

In theory, sustainable housing is about future forms of living. In reality, it deals with the application of state-of-the-art technologies to traditional typologies.

If one looks at the technologies and techniques currently applied in the field of sustainable architecture, it becomes evident that few of these actually have something to do with architecture as a space defining entity. The majority either deals with the application of external mechanical systems or learned behaviour patterns, but ultimately, neither of these two is immediately connected to architecture itself and could be applied independently from any specific typology.

Our project tries to prototypically examine how far space itself can help create an efficient sustainable single-housing unit without the immediate necessity for cutting-edge technologies. In doing so, we did not start from a fixed typology but rather tried to use the constraints imposed as a forming tool, thereby developing highly specialized phenotypes.

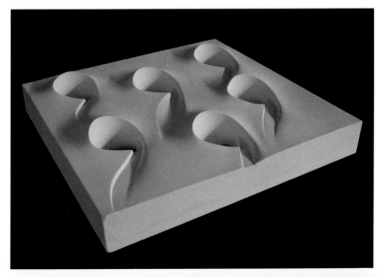

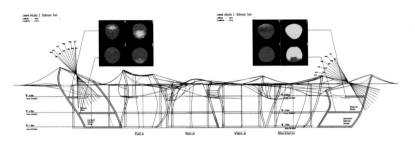

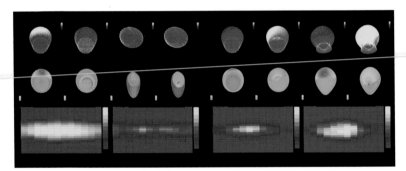

| Richard Garber
John Murphy | Architect | richard@emergence.net |
| | NA_USA | Columbia University |

The CommandPOD is a proposal for a rapidly deployable, performance-based structure designed to provide shelter to persons affected by natural disasters such as the South Asian tsunamis and Hurricane Katrina in the US. It can also provide habitation to explorers, surveyors, and scientists working in remote, hostile environments, ranging from the bitter cold of the Falkland Islands to the wind swept mountainous coast of Southern France and Catalonia. Design procedures owed much to an extensive research done in the area of contemporary naval architecture and construction. The customizable series of deployable modules that make up a single CommandPod are derived in concept from the dispersed fabrication of a United States Navy nuclear submarine, built in large mission-specific components in two disparate shipyards, coordinated by a single virtual model and built with advanced computer-numerically-controlled (CNC) fabrication techniques.

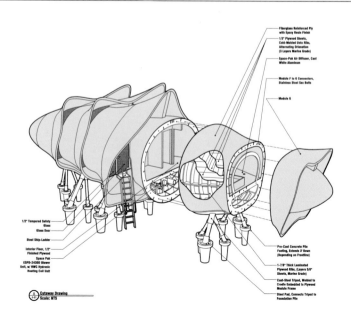

Cutaway Drawing
Scale: NTS

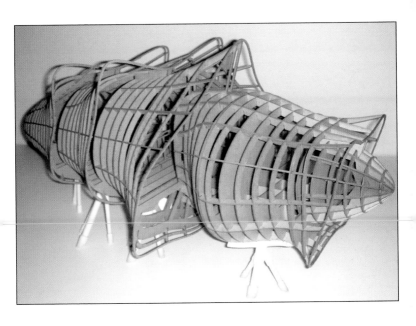

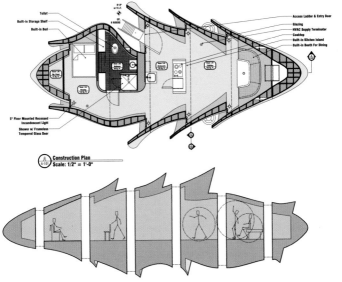

Construction Plan
Scale: 1/2" = 1'-0"

Toilet
Built-in Storage Shelf
Built-in Bed

Access Ladder & Entry Door
Glazing
HVAC Supply Terminator
Cooktop
Built-in Kitchen Island
Built-in Booth For Dining

5" Floor Mounted Recessed
Incandescent Light

Shower w/ Frameless
Tempered Glass Door

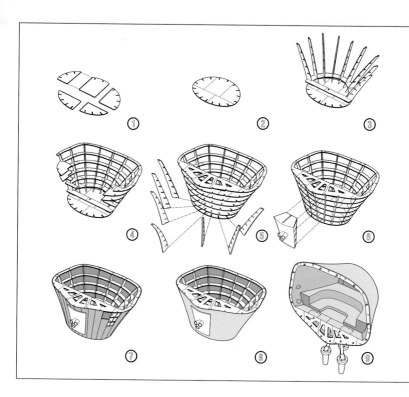

SITE A:

Potential Location:
North America,
Alaska
Junegu legion
Avg. Rainfall per Year: 55"
Avg. Temp. Range: 0°C - 13°C

Prevailing Site Conditions:

-Cool Temperature

-Dominated by North blowing local wind, the Taku, which reaches 77 Knots.

-The Taku is both cold and dry.

-Command Pod would be orientated North.

-The Command Pod can be placed in a location along the shoreline. If soil proves to be wet or clay-like, deeper piles or a floating foundation can be specified.

-The mission package of the Pod would require insulation and a smaller area of glazing.

SITE C:

Potential Location:
South America,
The Falkland Islands
Stanley Region
Avg. Rainfall per Year: 24"
Avg. Temp. Range: 2°C - 9.3°C

Prevailing Site Conditions:

-Extremely Cold Temperature

-Punctuated by the Pruga, a cold wind blowing down from the Andes Mtns to the West. Known to reach 110 Knots in magnitude.

-Command Pod would be orientated to the West, providing the least amount of surface area to the Pruga.

-The rocky, uneven terrain of the islands lends itself to the elevated tripod legs of the Command Pod.

-The mission package for a Command Pod deployed here would have to be practically self-sufficient.

52

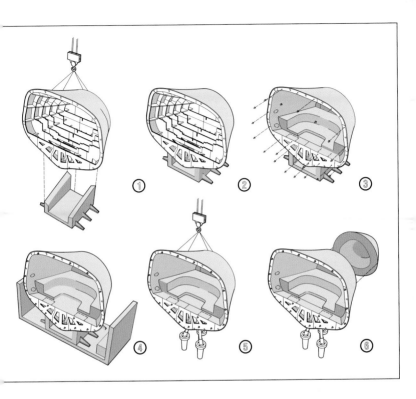

SITE B:

Potential Location:
Europe,
Provence/Catalonia
Marseilles Region
Avg. Rainfall per Year: 20"
Avg. Temp. Range: 8°C -
29°C

Prevailing Site Conditions:

-Warm during most of year.
Winter is punctuated by a
brutally cold Northwest wind,
the Mistral, reaching 80 knots.

-Command Pod would be
orientated Northwest to provide
a streamlined barrier to the
Mistral.

-The Command Pod can be sited
on the beach, requiring deeper
pile foundations than the normal
deployment outfit.

-Rural or isolated areas along
the shoreline necessitate a
plug-in sled to carry well
connections, an electrical
generator, and waste sewage
extraction.

SITE D:

Potential Location:
Asia,
Indian Sub-Continent
Calcutta Region
Avg. Rainfall per Year: 64"
Avg. Temp. Range: 18°C -
35°C

Prevailing Site Conditions:

-The Monsoon Wind, carries
heat, humidity, & rain during
the summer months westward
from the East.

-The Command Pod will be
orientated towards the East, to
combat the ill effects fo the
Monsoon.

-The Command Pod will be
orientated towards the East, to
combat the ill effects fo the
Monsoon.

-The cooling requirements can
be combined with natural
ventilation to regulate the
interior humidity of the Pod.

-Flooding is common, hence the
Command Pod entry level shoul:
be no less than 9' from the
ground level.

| Julian Pattison | Architect | julianhpattison@mac.com |
| | EU_UK | University of Greenwich |

MISSION The carapace project offers guest services & innovative resort accommodation in the unique and beautiful setting of the Sunshine Coast, British Columbia. We provide a relaxed and yet stimulating luxury environment developed solely on carefully researched sustainable principals and operated with minimal environmental impact.

THE IDEA behind The Carapace Project is to offer an alternative luxury environment, which is an immersive and authentic experience of nature and a retreat from the increasingly frantic, frenzied life of modern time. A series of tent like cocoon structures employing leading edge technologies, specially designed and locally fabricated will provide accommodation for couples, families and small groups. A singular lodge, simply constructed from locally sourced timber will provide dining, lounge and bar facilities. A series of bridge and deck like structures will link the cocoons, some at shore level, some elevated in the canopies of the old growth forest setting.

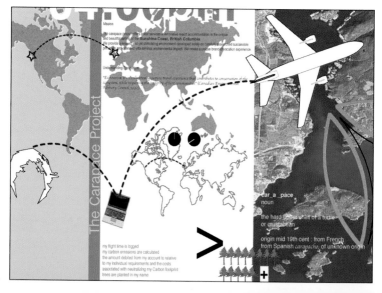

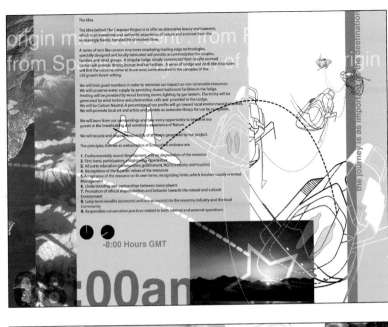

The Idea

The idea behind The Carapace Project is to offer an alternative luxury environment, which is an immersive and authentic experience of nature and a retreat from the increasingly frantic, frenzied life of modern time.

A series of tent like cocoon structures employing leading edge technologies, specially designed and locally fabricated will provide accommodation for couples, families and small groups. A singular lodge, simply constructed from locally sourced timber will provide dining, lounge and bar facilities. A series of bridge and deck like structures will link the cocoons, some at shore level, some elevated in the canopies of the old growth forest setting.

We will limit guest numbers in order to minimize our impact on non-renewable resources. We will conserve water supply by providing shared bathroom facilities in the lodge. Heating will be provided by wood burning stoves, lighting by gas lantern. Electricity will be generated by wind turbine and photovoltaic cells and provided in the Lodge. We will be Carbon Neutral. A percentage of our profits will go toward local environmental issues. We will promote local art and artists and provide an extensive library for use by our guests.

We will learn from our surroundings and take every opportunity to immerse our guests in the breathtaking and wondrous experience of Nature.

We will recycle and dispose responsibly of all waste generated by our project.

The principles, that we as ambassadors of Ecotourism embrace are:

1. Environmentally sound development and no degradation of the resource
2. First-hand, participatory, enlightening experiences
3. All party education (communities, government, NGOs, industry and tourists)
4. Recognition of the intrinsic values of the resources
5. Acceptance of the resource on its own terms, recognizing limits, which involves supply oriented Management
6. Understanding and partnerships between many players
7. Promotion of ethical responsibilities and behavior towards the natural and cultural Environment
8. Long-term benefits (economic and non-economic) to the resource, industry and the local Community
9. Responsible conservation practices related to both internal and external operations

-8:00 Hours GMT

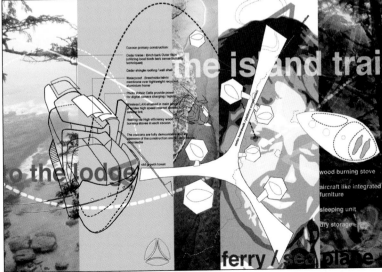

the island trail

Cocoon primary construction:

Cedar frame / Birch bark Outer Skin (utilizing local birch bark canoe building techniques)

Cedar shingle roofing / wall shell

Waterproof / Breathable fabric membrane over lightweight recycled aluminium frame

Photo Voltaic Cells provide power for digital camera charging / laptop

Wireless LAN ethereal in main lodge, provides high speed internet access via satellite link

Heating via High efficiency wood burning stove in each cocoon

The cocoons are fully demountable and all elements of the construction are bio-degradable / recyclable

old growth forest

wood burning stove

aircraft like integrated furniture

sleeping unit

dry storage

ferry / seaplane

1f437

ALG.AE

CH

Spiros I Papadimitriou Anastasia Tzaka	Architect	spiros_ip@yahoo.gr
	EU_Greece	Aristotle University of Thessaloniki

ALG.AE is a parametric adaptive inhabitation system which mimics sea-weed's ecology and structure. **ALG.AE** is a dynamic genotype unit system, capable of favouring varied combinations with adaptive behaviour and emerging properties. The **ALG.AE** is not regarded as a static and barrier building system but as a dynamic environmental filter, which manipulates the passage of energy flows in the form of light, heat, air and sound. It is designed and embedded with new technologies and it delivers a new aesthetic for architecture generating new unexpected forms and visual effects, Bio climatically devised, regionally based, technically competent, the peculiarity of the material system generates a range of possibilities in responding to the different requirements of structural, spatial and ergonomic adaptability. Changes range from 'local' manipulation of individual components, to the 'global' manipulation of component material systems.

ALG.AE is able to adjust to the different cultural structures and to adapt to a rich variety of uses. It is changes shape and content in real time achieving the reduction of buildings energy requirements.

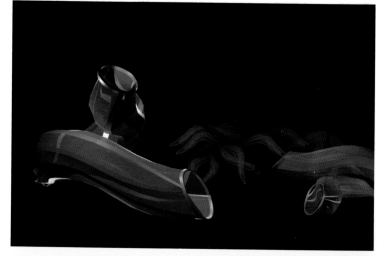

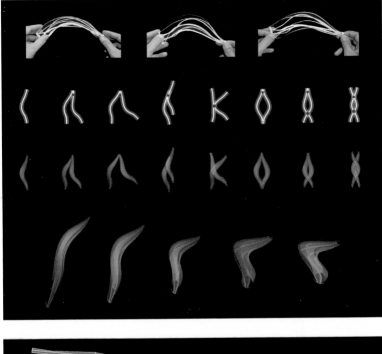

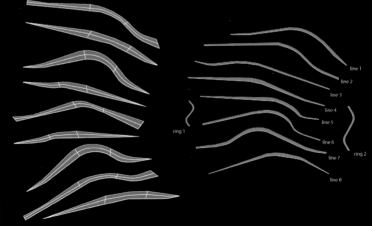

1ˢᵗ Prize Single Housing

| Gaetan Kohler | Student | kohler_gaetan@yahoo.fr |
| | EU_France | Ecole Spéciale d'Architecture |

The territory should be cautiously observed, studied, experienced, in order to be fully apprehended. The project requires a solution of continuity with what already composes the place but it shall not exclude original contributions. Constitutive elements of a contextual architecture: The building is conceived as an extension of the environment that surrounds it. The building structure is made of elements which are intrinsic to the site: water, straw, and earth-materials used in the rice terraces retaining walls. The flexible and evolving bamboo structure takes into account the human needs of space on the site. The envelope changes according to climatic variations. It expands in summer in order to ventilate the interior space and provide shade.
In winter, it contracts and acquires density so as to insulate the inhabitants against the cold and humidity. This is the simple property of the pinecone. The house has to contribute to the biological equilibrium of the site, as well as follow the rhythm of seasons and production.

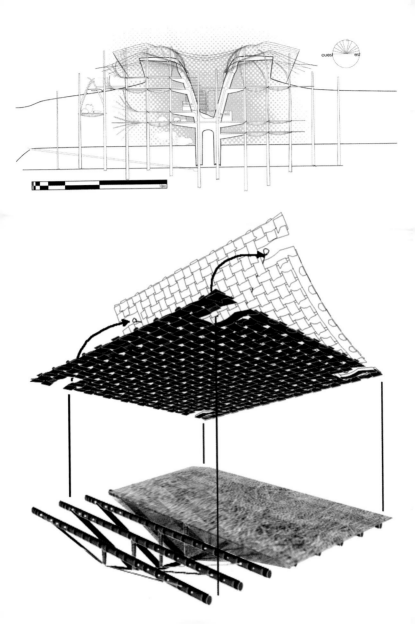

ouest   est

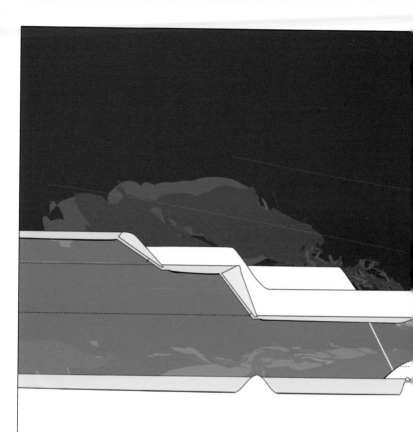

10m

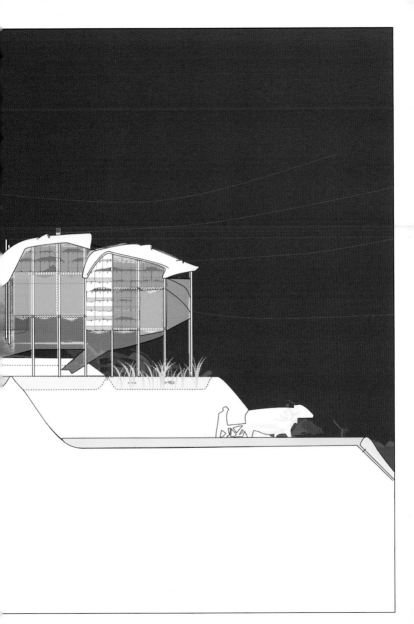

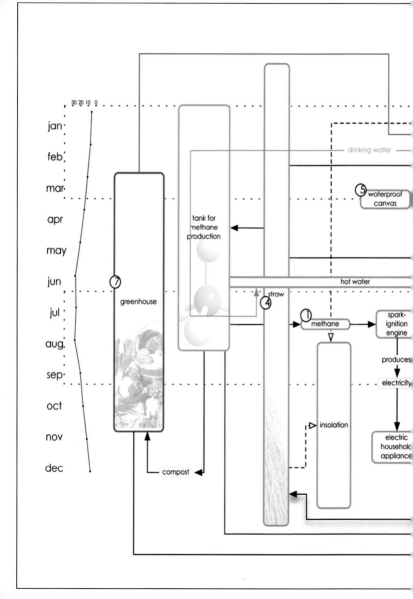

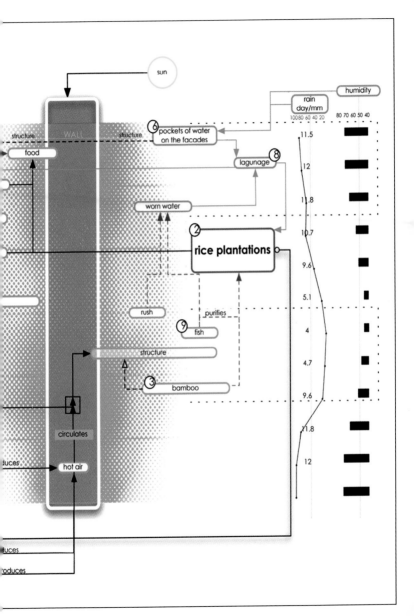

– Ricardo Arandia	– Architect	– ricardo.arandia@w2a.com.mx
– Alessandro Uras		
– Maria Ludovica Tramontin	– NA_Mexico	– Universidad Cristobal Colón
– Kristine Mun		

Instead of presenting an example of a self-sufficient building, we have chosen to show how a systematic set up can be applied such that a multiple housing complex could be developed under various climatic situations. We feel that this is critical for the research and that it can offer more information in the end. Our central focus is a system which results in an auto-sustainable building under several climates from the extreme arid climates to heavy precipitation to dry cold.

They are understood under categories of: 1– Energy conservation, 2– Formal/geometrical research and 3– (Flexible) programming. In addition, it should be understood that such a system can be set up wherein all three categories are developed simultaneously rather than in a typical segmented approach. In other words, as geometry is critical in the outcome to energy conservation (ex. orientation for shade, sunlight), program can be developed in parallel to the evolution of the geometry/structure.

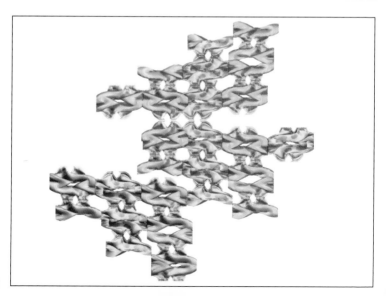

Species photo analysis

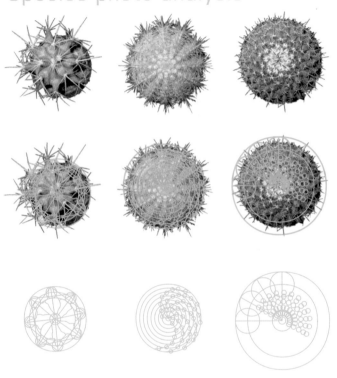

Increasing Profile System

$C^a = 30$
$C^b = 20$
$C^c = 30$
$C^d = 20$
$C^e = 30$
$C^f = 20$
$C^g = 30$

Scenario_01

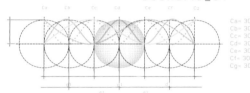

$Ca = 30$
$Cb = 30$
$Cc = 30$
$Cd = 30$
$Ce = 30$
$Cf = 30$
$Cg = 30$

Scenario_02

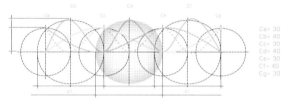

$Ca = 30$
$Cb = 40$
$Cc = 30$
$Cd = 40$
$Ce = 30$
$Cf = 40$
$Cg = 30$

Scenario_03

Joint each Profile

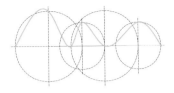
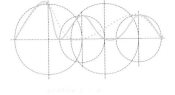

Bioclimatic System

general system

winter

summer day

summer night

f9008 Boomerang House

5H

- Laura Montanini
- Roberta Donsanti
- Fabiana Dore
- Francesco Pellisari

- Architect

- EU_Italy

- laura.montanini@tiscali.it

Flexibility is a central issue for our project, because it allows many usages and replacements in various contexts. **LOCATION** We chose a place already damaged by human activity: a mining cave. **THE PROJECT** Our proposal consists of a single-family unit composed of two aerodynamic volumes shaped to adapt to strong winds and also to fit into the ground. One is the living space; the other contains the technological installations and a small greenhouse. **TECHNOLOGICAL VOLUME** consists of a shell surface 138 m² raised at 2,5 m high and linked to the ground by a small greenhouse. This surface is made by two layers, one consisting of photovoltaic panels, the other one consisting of solar cylindrical panels. This particular shape follows the solar journey, with an efficiency of 22%. **HEATING SYSTEM** Inside the house we put a water wall. During the summer nights the water gets cold, and during the day, the water falls down the wall cooling the house.

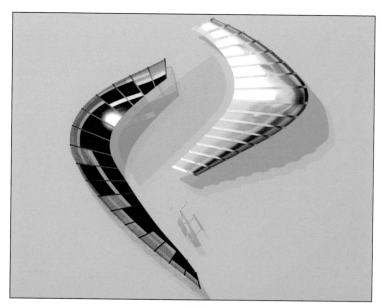

AIR CONDITIONING / HEATING WATER

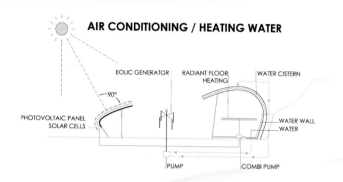

EOLIC GENERATOR

RADIANT FLOOR HEATING

WATER CISTERN

90°

PHOTOVOLTAIC PANEL
SOLAR CELLS

WATER WALL
WATER

PUMP

COMBI PUMP

BIOGAS AND DISPOSING OF RUBBISH

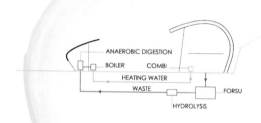

ANAEROBIC DIGESTION

BOILER   COMBI

HEATING WATER

WASTE

FORSU

HYDROLYSIS

ELECTRIC POWER

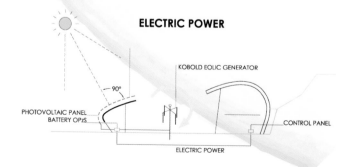

KOBOLD EOLIC GENERATOR

90°

PHOTOVOLTAIC PANEL
BATTERY OPzS

CONTROL PANEL

ELECTRIC POWER

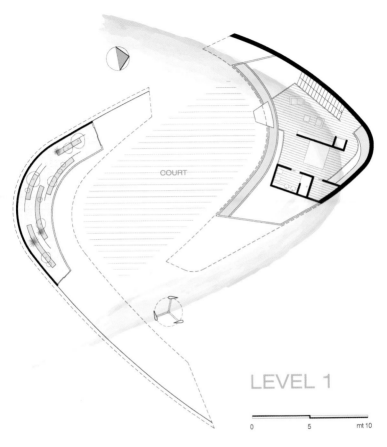

COURT

LEVEL 1

0   5   mt 10

─ Fareh Garba
─ Austin Seid

─ Architect   ─ vijaya.shankar@gmail.com

─ AF_Nigeria   ─ University of Pennsylvania

Calabar, a seaport of West Africa in the British protectorate of Southern Nigeria. The premise of this proposal is hinged on a sustainable solution to housing that lies effectively in our capability to access and manipulate the order and language of life at a scale otherwise uncharted and unexplored in the field of architecture. The initial scale of this idea lies at the molecular level, at the nexus of life and the environment; architecture must locate the rules of habitation within the seed of a species and allow it to germinate to execute these rules while responding to environmental factors, making decisions on the optimal responses to support human life.

PERFORMATIVE STRATEGIES Active structure [Below Ground] o Root hairs are responsible for probing environmental conditions and monitoring changes in that system. Root caps have the capability to communicate with each other and function to optimize structural bearing, nutrient intake, noxious particulate filtration, ground shielding, and armored defense of generative components. Active Structure [Above Ground] o Redundant vascular network responsible for the organic exchange of power, nutrient/gas/liquid exchange and communication networking/transmission.

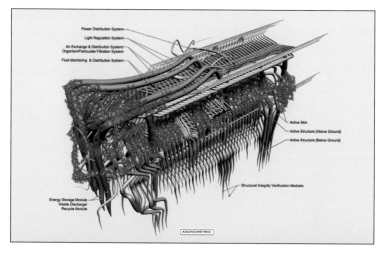

AXONOMETRIC

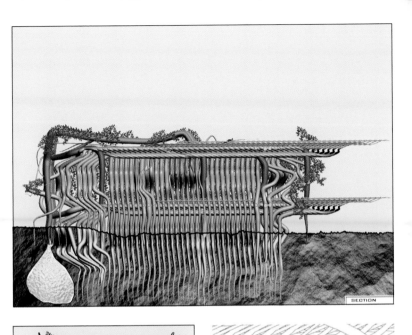

SECTION

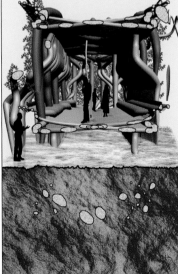

Blow and Form

Designed not just as a formal resource but as a more expansive category, Blow and Form, consistently optimistic and singular, is produced by modelling mechanisms that give off codes and applications contained in the dwelling in a forceful performance that is closely linked to the process of digital configuration. This process does not overlook the ecological impression it produces in terms of the administration of resources, energy use or social impact. It feeds on technological mechanisms for its self-sufficiency, imperceptible in its conception, suggesting at once growth and expansion, and explosion, mobility, centrifugation and animation that challenge the disciplinary statics of more normal architecture by means of the plural, kaleidoscopic approach of the configuration of the self-sufficient dwelling.

In Blow and Form, the approaches are produced by very differing viewpoints. This may involve elements that emphasise a communal wind-powered system, arranged to integrate into a potential larger-scale scenario, such as Aedex living unit. These mechanisms reproduce a map with an animal texture to constitute facings and successively optimize energy performance, and regulate water management in the form of Island, open to an archipelago-type reconfiguration. As a self-supporting vertical element that unfolds, like a body of revolution, it acquires a singular position in the territory, harnessing all possible natural resources, regulating thermal behaviour and allowing the possible inclusion of sustainable dwelling cells, Sunflower. In the form of small timber units, reminiscent of ship construction, floating and dirigible, it forms a fleet of boats with, perhaps a common destination.

Rather than being an isolated intervention, Blow and Form is mainly, but not exclusively, designed with a view to integration in a larger social element, as a part that blends into the crowd.

Whether the alternatives chosen are plural and distant or closely related and near at hand, they are not static but highly dynamic. They introduce the factors of time, expansion and movement into their conception. They are marked by the power of the form and produce a degree of excitation in the territory. By agitating it, they lend it an intensity that catalyses exchange, independently of the degree of sophistication of the setting.

3eaa9 Echinite 5H

| Martin Kim | Architect | www.interaction-architecture.com
kim@interaction-architecture.com |
| | EU_Germany | Technisvche Universität Darmstadt |

Mobile floating structure for holidays, emergency and expedition use for up to twelve people. To stay self-sufficient in very different environments requires a consequent strategy. This building uses every resource which is provided by the local environment. Energy is taken from wind, sun, water stream and biological waste. The possibility to dive allows the building to use the temperature range between air and water. Water is collected in huge freshwater tanks during the rainy seasons and last for about three months.

The fermented biological waste is used as fertilizer for the floating fields and waste water is cleaned by the floating biological cleaning pond. The whole structure can be folded to a compact unit and can be easily transported on water ways. The building offers two floors. The floor over sea level can be used as a terrace like space or as a winter garden; the submergeable floor houses the sleep and work spaces and a living and kitchen room.

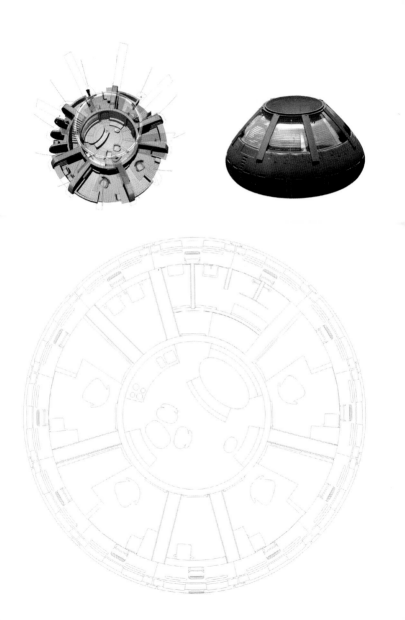

Julien Claude Jacquot | Student | jurian@fr.st

EU_France | Paris Malaquais

This project is based on a catastrophic scenario in the earth's future. It tries to display the paradox between evolution and technology.

3001: SEA ODYSSEY In this year, all the natural resources are depleted and planet Earth is covered by water. Humans have created a water world where they can not live. The first function of architecture was to protect its occupants; its new function is to feed its residents.

1- The Solar energy produces electricity which is stocked in a battery.

2- The envelope receives the water which is also stocked and distributed until the next rain.

3- Waste is cleaned, tried and mainly recycled.

4- Waste is burnt and the hot vapour isolated in battery.

5- The heat is distributed and sold through hot compressed air.

6- Organic waste is burnt to warm the building.

7- Excrements are sold to make manure for agriculture.

Finally the project uses technology as a translator of Nature.

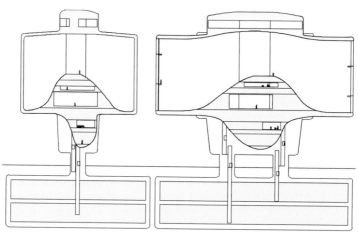

1. Local authorities   2. Housing area   3. 'downtown'   4. elevators   5. Reservoirs

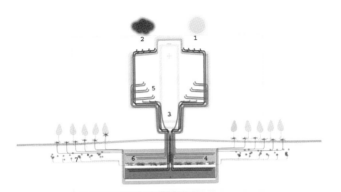

3f6d8 Saving Resources SH

- Mohamad Khabazi
- Sara Norouzi
- Keivan Saberi

- Architect
- AS_Iran

- memar_m@yahoo.com
- University of Mashhad

ENERGY RESOURCES Our strategy for supplying the electricity demands of the house is to provide solar batteries (photo-voltaic panels) for saving energy for a 24-hour use. For heating and cooling, according to the seasons and the climate we have made arrangements in design. Preparing septic tanks (Biogas) for using the recycled gas in winter and on the other hand wind tower fans for cooling in summer will help us minimize the use of energy. [Central courtyard – Thermal insulation – Shadings on facades]
MATERIALS RESOURCES Easily found materials in the surrounding environment. The main parts of materials needed for construction are supplied by recycled materials from the everyday garbage, and also arranging the gray water and bio-gas have emphasis on this method. Local materials like mat & plaster which are simply used in construction. [Using recycled beer bottles – Using concrete made of recycled materials – Using mat for roof covering and interior partitions]

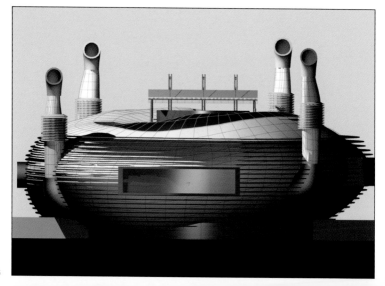

928e1 Lattice House

| Tom Warren Wiscombe | Architect | www.emergentarchitecture.com info@emergentarchitecture.com |
| | NA_USA | Emergent |

The Lattice House is a prototype based on the concept of the 'monocoque' structure, where hierarchical orders of skins, beams, columns, ducts, and passageways collapse into a 3-dimensional network defined by its coherence and unifying morphology. This network is defined by a system of IK handles, or 'bones' with a particular range of motion and adaptability.

The lattice is intended to perform simultaneously as primary structure and mechanical infrastructure: each segment of the armature will carry not only structural loads but will also be filled with water, creating a massive heat-exchange system capable of heating and cooling the space without the use of forced-air. This liquid system will be linked into an array of geothermal caissons reaching down into the bedrock for passive cooling.

This project is part of our office's continuing research on buildings which evolve, converge, and operate ecologically in the broadest sense.

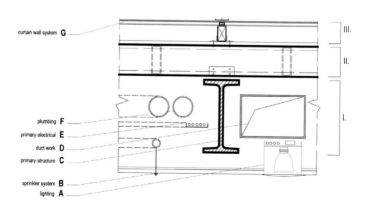

curtain wall system **G**

plumbing **F**
primary electrical **E**
duct work **D**
primary structure **C**

sprinkler system **B**
lighting **A**

III.

II.

I.

Striated Infrastructural System
- distinct layers with dedicated functions (1-3)
- no feedback

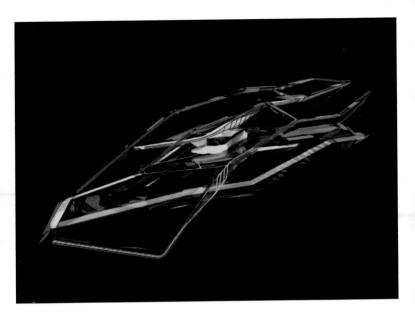

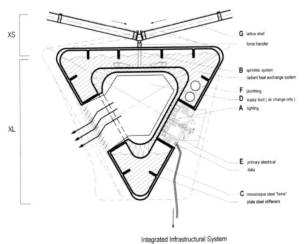

XS

XL

G lattice shell
force transfer

B sprinkler system
radiant heat exchange system

F plumbing
D suppy duct (air change only)
A lighting

E primary electrical
data

C monocoque steel "bone"
plate steel stiffeners

Integrated Infrastructural System
- highly differentiated
- dissolving of secondary   layers (2)
- feedback between systems

2981f Fighting Abandonment SH

- Pedro Bento | - Architect | - pedroduartebento@mail.pt
| - EU_Portugal | - Universidade Técnica de Lisboa

The choice of the "single house unit" stands on the idea of designing a House for a middle-aged couple and provides contact with nature, agriculture and ecological environment on a self-sufficient way.

The specific site location, for the implantation of the prototype, is the open country, 8 km distant of Santa Isabel village center (population 650).

This village is located in central Alentejo and belongs to the regional district of Évora, Portugal.

ENERGETIC SUPPORT:

–Eolic generator, with a rational use of storage batteries, a full recovery of energy even with reduced wind speed and an inverter-box that transforms it for the domestic use.

–Solar panel (10 m²), pointed south and with an inclination of 30°, provides 1400 Kwh/year.

–Water Tanks to store rain water. The water to supply domestic use is conducted to an osmosis-inverse manual filter and re-conducted to the house. There's also a tank that stores the irrigation water.

–Vegetable garden, 100 m² of earth provides 130 kg tomato/year; 94 kg potato/year; 60 kg beans/year; 144 kg watermelon/year.

–Chicken yard, 10 chickens provides 2250 eggs/year and recycles the organic food garbage.

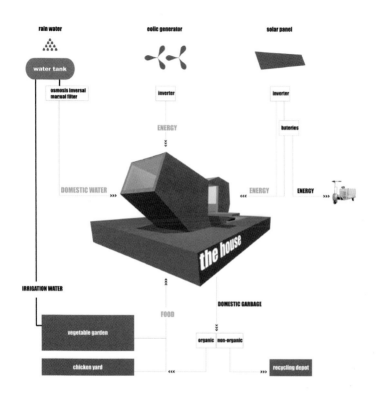

rain water

water tank

osmosis inversal
macual filter

eolic generator

inverter

ENERGY

solar panel

inverter

bateries

DOMESTIC WATER

ENERGY

ENERGY

the house

IRRIGATION WATER

DOMESTIC GARBAGE

FOOD

vegetable garden

organic   non-organic

chicken yard

recycling depot

SECTION

3.6	**ab34d**	**Nomad Refuge**	**SH**

Michael Vargas Moya	– Architect	– pachacamac@hotmail.com
	– SA_ Peru	– MVM architects

This refuge uses recycled materials that can be recycled several times as the steel of an old car or old newspapers which can be transformed into structures or borders. The refuge is a blossom that moves away from the floor and leaves a green zone under the building reducing the effects of the thermal inertia of the ground. The recycled structure is supported by a pentagonal sequence structure in which every part is connected with 3 points and it gives a continuous balancing state with continuous borders that can be modified according to the movement of the sun and allows a better use of the diffuse radiation and natural convective ventilation. The refuge has a purge zone which is connected to a biogas dome that ferments the waste and to a tank that treats the black waters. All these strategies reduce the contamination by reutilizing the resources and transform the refuge into a new way of understanding the environment.

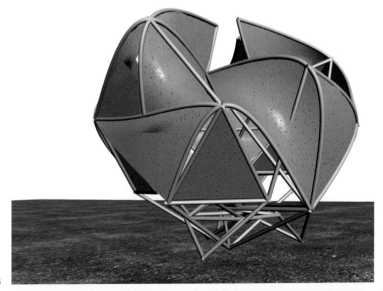

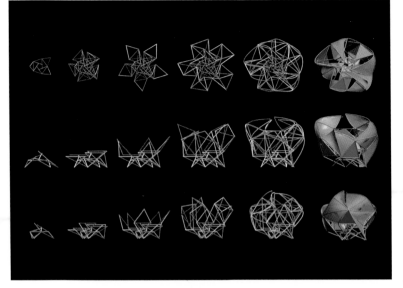

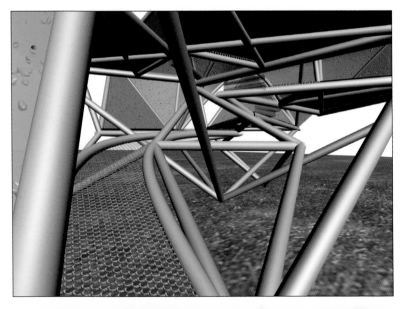

efafs ['instinkt]

 SH

| –Tom Forster
–Nadine Lachmund
–Christian Raschke
–Marko Schneider | – Student

– EU_Germany | – 4aus49@web.de

– FH Erfurt |

Our proposal, an organic form, has the intention of using high-surface in producing energy as well as integration to environment. The outer shape is defined by the natural principle of increasing the surface, according to the human intestine. Convexities along straight lines imparts the primary surface in a multiple way. Thereby it accrues a large potential in gaining solar energy. The conception of a flexible membrane, which reacts according to climatic changes by using their different functions, supplies energy to the housing and guarantees its independence. The elastic structure allows an assembly on nearly every building-shape. Our suggestion, covering an organic form with the membrane, is only one possibility using the advantages of this membrane. The membrane, called ['instinkt], transforms solar energy into electric power, uses sunbeams for water heating, collects rainwater, produces electric energy by using the wind-generator and cools down the housing by using phasing changing material.

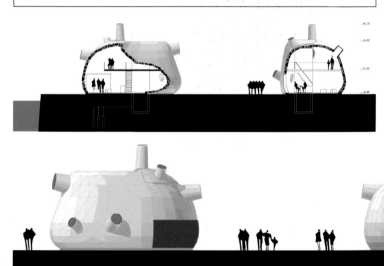

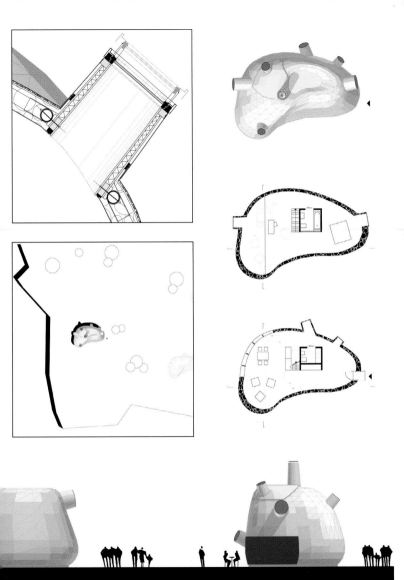

- Alberto Lara
- Paula Veronica
- Nogueron Madrid

- Student

- ablp@yahoo.com

- NA_Mexico

- ITESM camups Queretaro

ADEX: ADAPT structure to site, DEFORM space with program, EXPOSE systems to events. ADEX is prefabricated module-based living unit. The construction and energy-resource systems contemplate ADEX's adaptation to any given site in which its structure might be supported. This living unit absorbs and recycles the resources or wastes available whether in its manufacturing process or during its inhabitation use. The construction system can be located and relocated anyplace allowing it to adapt to an evolving program, where an expansion or reduction of spaces is required. ADEX takes advantage of the surfaces, edges and nodes inherent of the structure in order to use them for the distribution of services through out the living unit delivering them to the specific points where they'll be used. ADEX is an open system that states the basis for a broad-range construction system meant to be developed as it brings together human comfort at any location or circumstance with sustainable design.

8b8db Sunflower Project 5H

| Predrag Djermanovic | Architect | pedjamt@ptt.yu |
| Tatic Nina | EU_Serbia & Montenegro | Faculty of Architecture Belgrade |

The idea of "the sunflower" project is to make several similar units of houses connected to infrastructure by a main "core". This self-sufficient system takes only indispensable resources (solar energy, rainwater). The system generates recyclable waste with mechanisms on underground level. The units are connected in underground level by canals attached to the elevator core. The roof is designed for collecting rainwater in a reservoir and with proper solar panels used for a system heating.

The core is made of segments that can rotateg 360°,along a horizontal axis so that the units attached to them can follow the movement of the sun and reasorb its energy. The housing units are attached to rotatable core segments, very easy to detach. They have rotatable roof solar panels, moving roof slabs and sliding and rotating facade panels (parts are photo-sensitive), open interior space with sliding panels (free organizable interior). The installation is positioned in two zones:

1- Suspended ceiling (air conditioning system, technical installations).
2- floor (heating, plumbing elements, electrical installations).

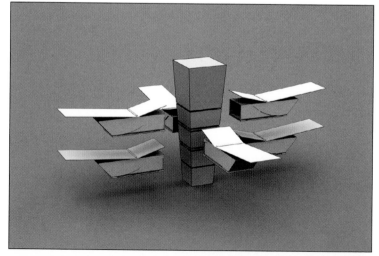

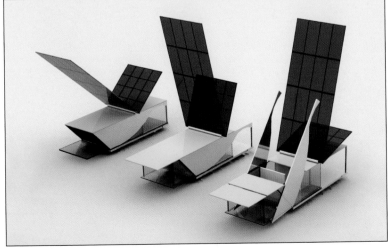

22f8d

Skplbdspb2

 SH

| -Lodes Vranken
-Kitty Strybol
-Jan Vermeylen | - Architect | - lode.vranken@telenet.be |
| | - EU_Belgium | - Hogeschool voor Wetenschap & Kunst, Sint-Lucas, Gent |

The Skplbdspb2 is a sensitive, kinetic passive house that responds to the use of its inhabitants. Normally houses are 50% or less occupied. In this project sensors are used to follow the uninhabited and adjust the space in the building to the needs of the users.

The house has a fixed core where technical functions are located. Around this core, a moving structure defines the other rooms. Used spaces will expand, while the unused area is compressed, thus saving energy. The load bearing structure is a dome structure, made of telescopic tubes, with a pneumatic system of Fluidic Muscles attached inside, creating a kinetic building. The walls are made of a rubber skin, filled with 40 cm insulating cellulose flakes, making the walls flexible and adaptive to the use of the building.

A thermal solar system stores warm water in a boiler during summertime, for heating during wintertime. The building is covered with a PV solar foil, to generate electricity and hydrogen gas.

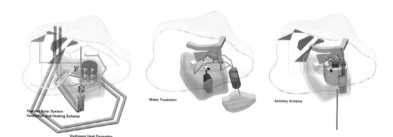

Thermal Solar System
Ventilation and Heating Scheme

Water Treatment

Sanitary Scheme

Hydrogen Heat Generator

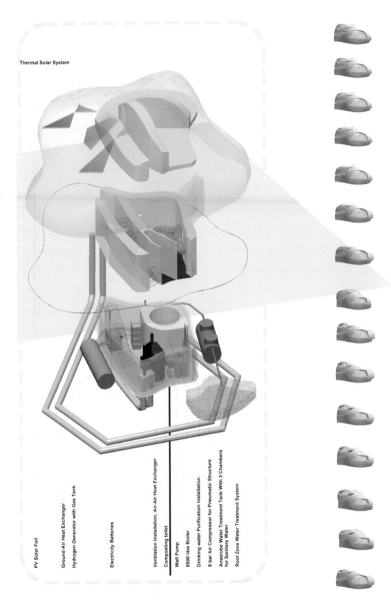

Thermal Solar System

PV Solar Foil

Ground-Air Heat Exchanger

Hydrogen Generator with Gas Tank

Electricity Batteries

Ventilation Installation, Air-Air Heat Exchanger

Composting toilet

Well Pump

8500 litre Boiler

Drinking water Purification Installation

8 bar Air Compressor for Pneumatic Structure

Anaerobe Water Treatment Tank With 3 Chambers for Sanitary Water

Root Zone Water Treatment System

350a0 Biodynamic House SH

Ricardo Zaldivar Armenta	Architect	zaldivar@arqa.com
	NA_Mexico	ZAR arquitectos

The same way flowers receive their nutriments this house takes its energy. It has a concept that is related to the inhaling and exhaling (IN-OUT), the processes of the metamorphosis of a biotic element present themselves when the house receives water, light and air.

The design is based on the logic of interconnecting the ecologic energy systems (water, sun, wind and soil) with biologic systems (plants as nutriments and as construction material, animals as nutriments and as working form and the human being) thus creating permanent cycles and establishing successions of the different functions.

Each element fulfills more than one use and the important functions are supported by various elements. The house establishes working relationships between each element of which it is composed. This way the necessities of each element are covered by the functions of the other ones.

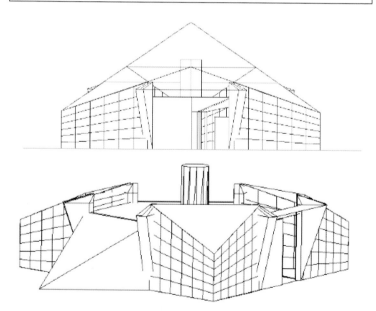

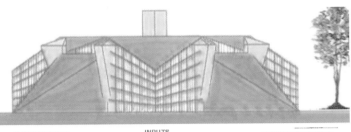

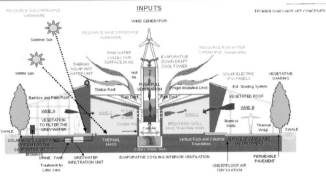

INPUTS

RESOURCE SUN 2 PRINCIPLE: Sustainability

TECHNOLOGIES NOT YET CONCEIVED

WIND GENERATOR

Sommer Sun

Winter Sun

RESOURCE WIND 3 PRINCIPLE: Sustainability

RESOURCE RAIN WATER 1 PRINCIPLE: Sustainability

RAIN WATER COLLECTION SURFACE 90 m2

EVAPORATIVE DOWN-DRAFT COOL TOWER

THERMO SOLAR HOT WATER UNIT

Hot Air

PUSH-PULL VENTILATION

SOLAR ELECTRIC (PV) PANELS

VEGETATIVE SHADING

Timber Roof

Rigid Insulation Deck

Ext. Shading System

Bamboo and Palm Roof

Rain Duct

Rain Duct

VEGETATED ROOF

WIND A

WIND C

WIND C

WIND B

VEGETATION TO FILTER THE GREYWATER

Air Duct

In Draft

Breathing Wall Micro Straw Bale Walls

Thermal Wrap

SWALE

Trombe Wall

Bamboo Walls

SWALE

SOLAR WASTE CONTAINER SYSTEM FOR THE COMPOSTING OF THE BIOMASS

THERMAL MASS

Cool Air

Vertical Rock and Columns Foundation

NATIVE GRASSES AND WILDFLOWERS

URINE TANK Treatment for Citric Tree

GREYWATER INFILTRATION UNIT

Cistern Water: Rain

EVAPORATIVE COOLING INTERIOR VENTILATION

UNDERFLOOR AIR CIRCULATION

PERMEABLE PAVEMENT

EVAPORATIVE COOLING INTERIOR VENTILATION

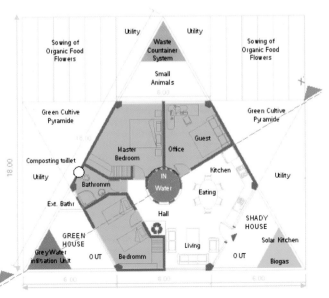

	Utility	Waste Countainer System	Utility	
Sowing of Organic Food Flowers		Small Animals		Sowing of Organic Food Flowers
Green Cultive Pyramide				Green Cultive Pyramide
	Master Bedroom	Office	Guest	
Composting toillet		IN Water	Kitchen	
Utility	Bathromm		Eating	Utility
Ext. Bathr		Hall		SHADY HOUSE
GREEN HOUSE	OUT		Living	Solar Kitchen
GreyWater infiltration Unit	Bedromm	OUT		Biogas

e2edd | The Jalousie House | 5H

| –Nikita V. Barinov –Komba Bakh | – Architect | – kombabakh@mail.ru | |
| | – EU_Russia | – IGASA, Russia | |

The house design was based on the "sunflower" principle of. As the sunflower follows the sun during a day, so does the house.

The defending constructions of the house are built so that they capture the sun movement. They look like jalousie of different sizes, opening in different surfaces. They allow the sunlight to penetrate into the house. At the same time the jalousie can accumulate the sun energy. Owing to this energy the house can exist autonomously. The house is supplied by water with the help of a separate borehole which is under the house.

Water is rising up to the upper floor with the pump working from the sun energy. The water is passing through the wall which has the form of a hollow transparent construction.

Then the water falls down. This "artificial water-fall" rotates a mini-turbine which also produces power in winter period, when there is no sun.

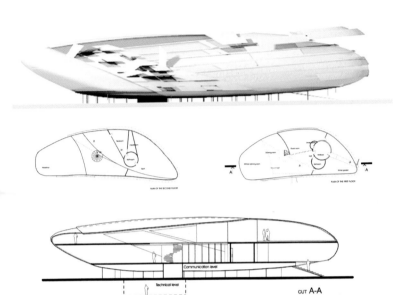

PLAN OF THE SECOND FLOOR

PLAN OF THE FIRST FLOOR

Communication level

Technical level

47 000

CUT A-A

Common and Related

4.1	2c35a	Under-space
4.2	3fa1f	T²Ower
4.3	5b98f	House in Bangladesh
4.4	5bad8	Micro Urban Habitat
4.5	6ceca	Post Tsunami Village
4.6	44fab	Super Châlet
4.7	193e6	NOAH's autARK
4.8	229d4	Urban Green
4.9	3685c	Radial High-Rise
4.10	a639c	Ecosystem (RE)Generator
4.11	b394d	Urban Sustainable
4.12	b5764	Cooperative Housing
4.13	d701a	Urban Gadgets
4.14	f33a2	Urban Rhizome
4.15	feb35	Vertical Communities
4.16	b8fbd	Housing in Tel-Aviv
4.17	0e724	Hybrid Tower
4.18	4327e	Housing in Montreal
4.19	d18f5	Zoom-House
4.20	e5600	Regenerating Hubs
4.21	09a26	Brazil Built
4.22	83a3c	Ecosystem Injections 1st prize Collective Housing

The Self-Sufficient Housing Contest was divided into two main categories. A scale dichotomy included at once a self-sufficient single housing competition and a self-sufficient collective housing competition. In Collective, the self-sufficient house voluntarily subordinates itself to the whole, to the higher social entity of which it forms part, to the collective block of which it is a constituent body. While the primary aim of the dwelling is to be self-sufficient, independently of whether it fits into a larger collective apparatus, the ultimate defining objective of Collective, in all cases from the viewpoint of a highly optimistic social stance, is to integrate and address the block as a whole and to model the public space it generates, while its impact, in terms of the scale of intervention, has the greatest possible repercussion on the city.

Examples of this taxonomy are Service towers

and Ecosystem injections, the winner of first prize in the Self-Sufficient Collective Housing Contest.

Ecosystem injections, an interesting and outstanding entry, proposes the self-sufficiency of a system of multiple scales in three successive steps. The first is the appropriate choice of a setting for its social, cultural and energetic qualities; the second is the insertion of three artificial ecosystems into the city as a project strategy, and the third is the construction of three wrapped towers (see Wrapped) of hybrid ecological dwellings that activate nodes in different parts of the city, reconfiguring a larger territory.

The complex of dwellings piled up to form towers achieves self-sufficiency by means of the process of reception, storage and recycling of resources that occurs both within them and in the overall building of which they form part.

Between them, the towers manage their resources in a dynamic of collaboration-compensation-fusion.

They then extend some of their products to other towers, or other nodes, by means of administration points that weave a subsequent network, harnessing and promoting the high-level efficiency of the collective system. It proposes, then, an unlimited series of service towers according to the needs of the setting into which it is introduced.

The buildings comprise a vertical recycling structure that houses environmental service and conditioning mechanisms in its mutable skin, as well as rainwater collectors and wind generators, with public surfaces and dwellings (boxes for activities) inside.

The collective system may therefore be extended over the territory depending on local demand and need.

— Sung-Yong Park | — Student | — psy@vt.edu

| — AS_South Korea | — Virginia Tech, USA

In a sense, machines like airplanes and ships are more efficient in space wise. Before architects worked out a roof garden, a roof space was already well used as a deck in a ship. In a ship, almost residential spaces are located under a deck. A deck rather than the surface of water (or ground) is the line deciding "under" and "over". Thus, we can control a line, and "under-space" doesn't mean any more the space that has no sunrays and outside views. Interestingly, the shape of a ship, invented for the buoyancy of water, is also good for the floating units to use "air" and "sun". The ship-like shape of each unit helps sunrays to reach into the unit below and penetrate deep into the space through its roof garden. And the ship-like shape following fluid dynamics activates airflows for wind power generators: Venturi effect.

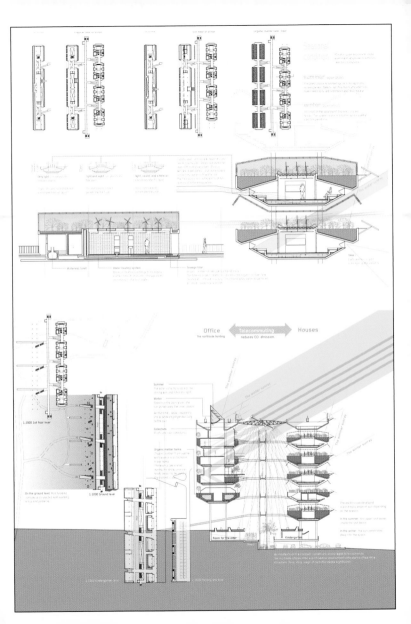

Office ←→ Telecommuting ←→ Houses

| –Damien Mikolajczyk | – Student | – 3damien@gmail.com |
| | – EU_France | – Ecole d'Architecture de Nancy |

What is the cheapest dwelling in all the ways? A tent. Which configuration can save both energy, green spaces, network needs? The tower.

Based upon this statement, T²ower, the Textile Tower, consists of a central metallic core for human flows on which modular egg-shaped flats are plugged, alternating with terraces. The whole is surrounded by a textile skin which is acting, with each egg's skin, like a double skin, to create a huge thermal insulation and regulation space as well as a great inside-out common space. The tubular structure of the central core integrates all the networks, and provides connection from flats to sustainable energy producing systems like the underground kernel, combining geothermal electricity and water recycling abilities.

The use of different materials, the energetic system, conciliates self-sufficiency both with a strong architecture and with building and social ideas: large spaces, a customizable textile skin, the freedom of the shape, an ecological building birth and death.

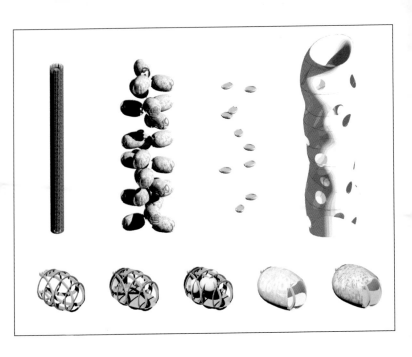

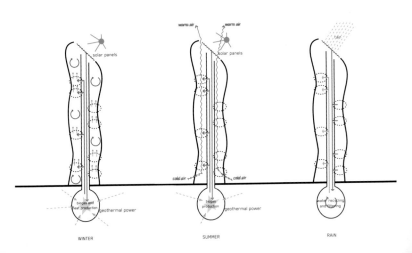

WINTER

SUMMER

RAIN

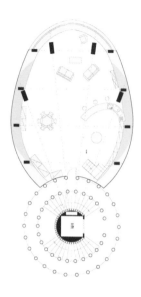
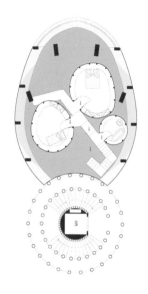

| | Sb98f | House in Bangladesh | CH |

| Nigel Craddock | Architect | nigel.craddock@pascalls.co.uk |
| | EU_UK | Sullivan Craddock Architects |

The project is designed to house a community of approximately 160 people in a land area that is calculated to support an autonomous food supply, provide the basis for economic development and a self sufficient renewable and passive energy strategy. An indispensable fact of sustainable design is renewable energy; in place of fossil fuels and high residential density over singular one off dwellings. The basis for the scheme is to embrace culture, nature, transport, materials, food and water supply, waste, equity and health a happiness in order to suggest a model to achieve a global sustainable future. In this sense the site context actively shapes and drives the design generators, the living condition and the ecological and economic imperatives. By integrating landscaping, climatic data, materials and vernacular types with the needs of community the scheme aspires to act as a microcosm of global holistic living.

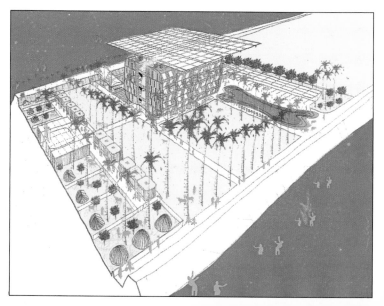

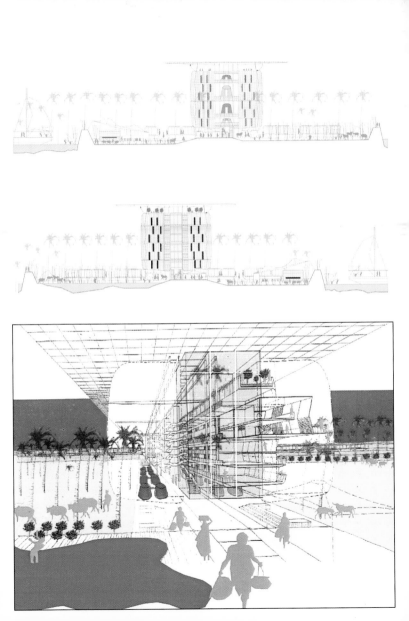

Sbad8

Micro Urban Habitat CH

- Lucas Martin Ruarte
- Fabiana Agusto
- Matteo Ferrari
- Anna Malaguti
- Francesco Tosi
- Alberto Verde

- Architect

- SA_Argentina

- www.artanestudio.net
- artanestudio@arq.net.ar

- ARTAN

Our proposal creates a habitat of sustainable collective housing, considering the relationship which a house has with its surrounding. A sustainable environment is synthesized in the result of a balance within ecological, economic and social indicators. Our hypothesis is based on the transferring of data into urban and architectural spaces through the materialization, the stratification of these numbers. The analysis started from an urban scale since the city is an "urban ecology". The objective is originating rule systems which work in different scenarios. The proposal considers the indicators in urban scale compared with those thought as projected in micro scale, aiming to create a sustainable collective system from the environment to the houses.

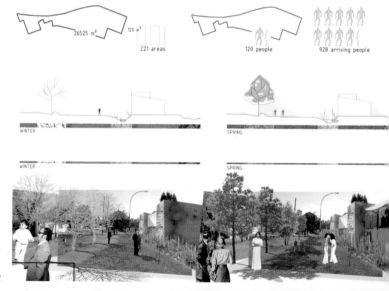

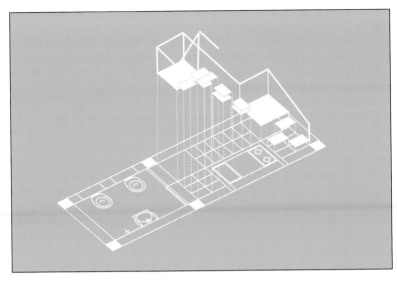

91 trees   309 necessary trees   1,2 car/family   264 cars | 4752 m² parking

SUMMER   AUTUMN

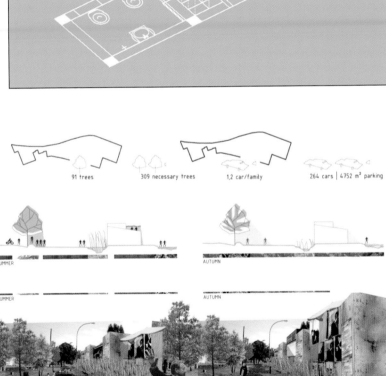

SUMMER   AUTUMN

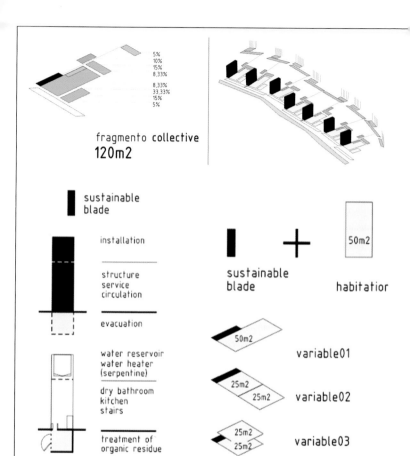

5%
10%
15%
8,33%

8,33%
33,33%
15%
5%

fragmento **collective**
120m2

sustainable blade

installation

structure
service
circulation

evacuation

water reservoir
water heater
(serpentine)

dry bathroom
kitchen
stairs

treatment of
organic residue

sustainable blade $+$ 50m2 habitation

50m2 — variable01

25m2 / 25m2 — variable02

25m2 / 25m2 — variable03

social
ED.01
ED.02

education

23,7% commercial
22,3% social service
13,8% artisans
8,9% builder
4,5% administration
13% other

541175 workers

215000 students

883 cultural b

social
VL.01
VL.02

violence   VL.01

2784 crimes against the property

segre

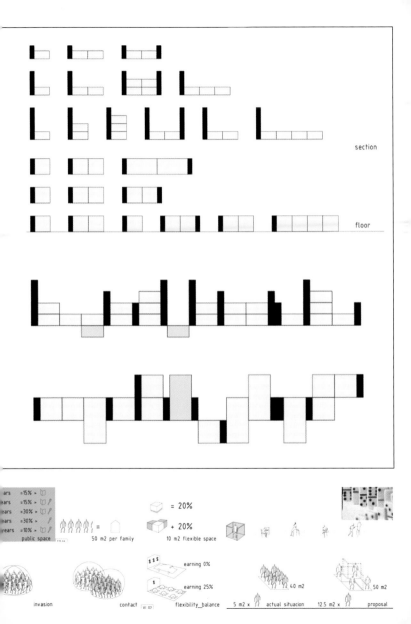

section

floor

ars   =15% ►
ears   =15% ►
ears   =30% ►
ears   =30% ►
years =10% ►
       public space   50 m2 per family

= 20%

+ 20%
10 m2 flexible space

earning 0%

earning 25%

invasion   contact   flexibility_balance   5 m2 x actual situacion   12.5 m2 x proposal

4.0 m2   5.0 m2

| –Joseph Ee Man Lim | –Archi– | –www.josephlimdesigns.com
–akilimem@nus.edu.sg |
| | –AS_Singapore | –Heriott-Watt University |

The provision of shelter is not enough when it is considered as a stand alone solution for the proud Acehnese people who are used to ways of life closely related to the land and the sea. Rebuilding must be considered in terms of continued relationships between livelihoods, environment and infrastructure; in ways which preserve tradition and culture without hindering progress or further damaging the environment.

It is in this context that the proposal for a 1000 inhabitant in a 5 hectare plot of land in inland Aceh Besar proposes a physical plan to sustain the economic recovery of the people whilst creating spaces for community living and dealing with waste management creatively.

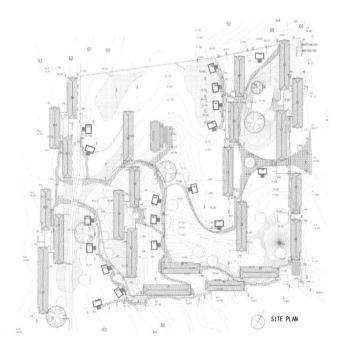

SITE PLAN

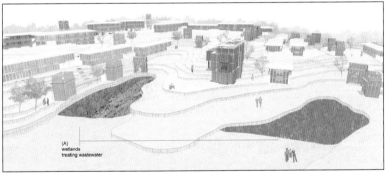

(A)
wetlands
treating wastewater

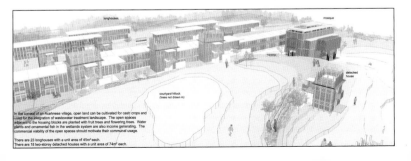

longhouses

mosque

detached house

courtyard hillock
(trees not drawn in)

In the context of an Acehnese village, open land can be cultivated for cash crops and used for the integration of wastewater treatment landscape. The open spaces adjacent to the housing blocks are planted with fruit trees and flowering trees. Water plants and ornamental fish in the wetlands system are also income generating. The commercial viability of the open spaces should motivate their communal usage.

There are 23 longhouses with a unit area of 45m² each.
There are 18 two-storey detached houses with a unit area of 74m² each.

- Walter Alberto Sanchez - Mauricio Sommacal - Mercedes Cuenca - Armando Perez Moreno	- Archi- - SA_Argentina	- www.futuraplanta.com.ar - futuraplanta@gmail.com - Futuraplantabureau

THE CONCENTRATION A concentration process is needed, defining and identifying use zones and leisure spaces, creating new and exciting shapes of living, purposely freeing nature and concentrating dynamically what's left for humans, a human nature of sorts.

By maximizing the local chalet to the size of "big villa", and rotating it "upside down" a new typology emerges: a housing building where the project's logics are inverted; maximizing instead of miniaturizing so as to generate the super size of collective dwellings; rationalization instead of excess for a maximal self-sufficiency.

The new super-chalet is a catalogue, of the rationalized elements of a traditional house but monumentalized to the size of collective dwellings to satisfy the human desire.

WATER CYCLE The pool on the roof works as a dike of rain water that immediately falls over a 15 meter high wall, becoming hydroelectric energy to aliment the elevators of the super-chalet, then part of the water is relocated on the cistern next to the pool providing grey water for the building's toilets and the refilling of the pool.

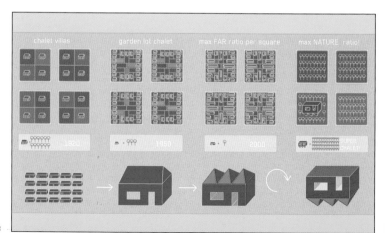

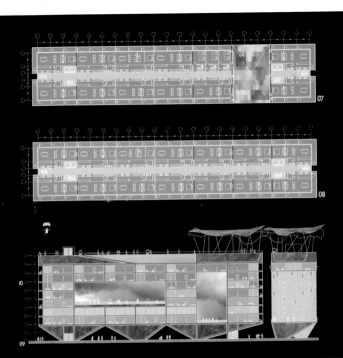

07

08

10

09

- Daniele Wagner
- Toshiya Kurihara
- Oliver Wildpaner
- Erich Ranegger

- Architect

- EU_Italy

- info@danielewagner.eu

- ISACF La Cambre, Belgium

Animals will provide the necessary primary energy in form of biogas and indirectly by waste heat. Their excrements will be used for plants that will grow faster because of the waste heat they will receive from the biogas plant. The plants will filter rain providing drinkable water. The plants will function as green filter. Their biomass will provide another source for energy. Their fruits, as well as the meat of the animals, will be consumed by the inhabitants or sold in shops, creating social connections. Harvested rainwater will be, as long as possible, recycled through plants. Exporting and selling what the system produces will permit to buy and import the necessary animal food. All what the building would produce would come back to it, imitating thus the process and the cycles of nature.

| Kalpesh Ramesh Solaniki | Architect | archsolanki@sify.com |
| | AS_India | Studio Solaniki |

'Urban Green' is an attempt to infuse a self-sustainable Architectural pattern in the contemporary urban scenario.

The city in focus for this particular project was Mumbai, situated on the west coast of Maharashtra sate in India.

The design tools consisting of a Green-Skin, Core, Buffer and Connectors were each clubbed with one or more predefined set of eco tools. Besides introducing energy efficiency, the idea was also to create an interface for the neighbourhood to understand the positive environmental and visual impact of this building on the surroundings.

Such architectural prototypes could become harbingers of a new self sustaining architectural vocabulary in the urban setup.

ELEVATION:

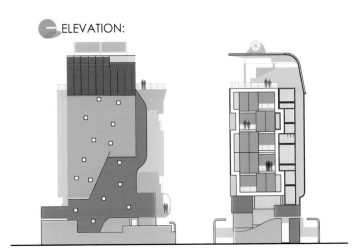

SOUTH ELEVATION   WEST ELEVATION

3685c Radial High-Rise CH

| Roberto Requejo | Architect | robertorequejo@hotmail.com |
| | EU_Spain | Cornell University + Columbia University |

Human behaviour plays a large part in adapting environments to make them comfortable throughout the year. Seasonal internal migration would serve as a passive strategy to adapt to changing temperatures within the thermal range provided by the dwelling. The thermal range within the unit is created through the radial organization of areas with varying degrees of exposure to the elements. The outer-most disc is seen as a balcony with high exposure to solar gain and loss. It is shown using both a mechanical strategy for solar gain (solar panels) and a passive method (thermal gain). The solar panels exist in the form of oval inserts onto the exposed outer surface. In contrast, the interior is massive with a high thermal gain value. Each unit makes use of a thermally massive south-facing beak. A retractable greenhouse film can be lowered to retain thermal gain during cold months or can be drawn back for maximum ventilation during higher temperatures.

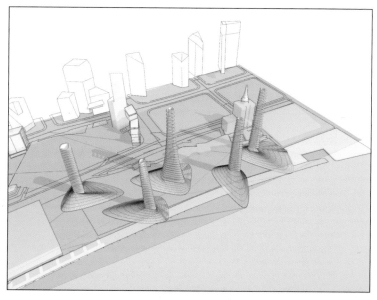

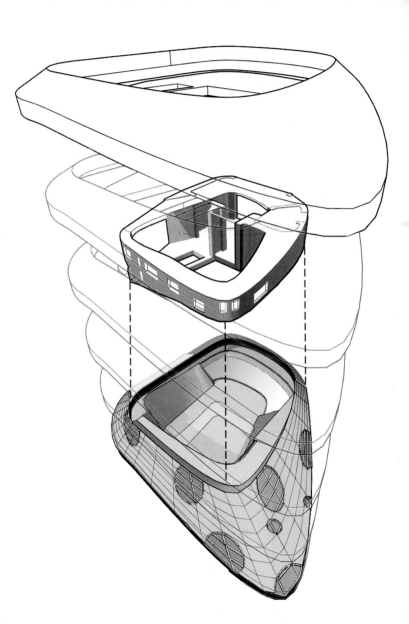

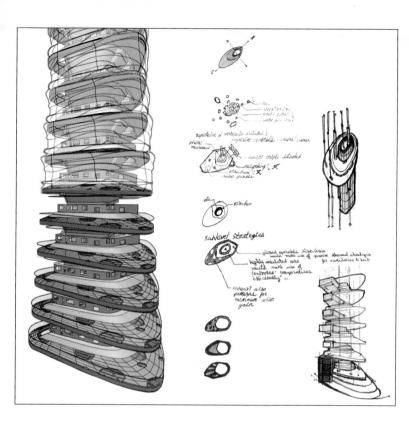

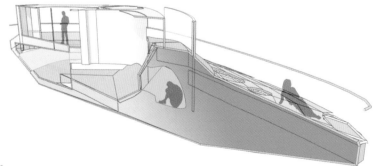

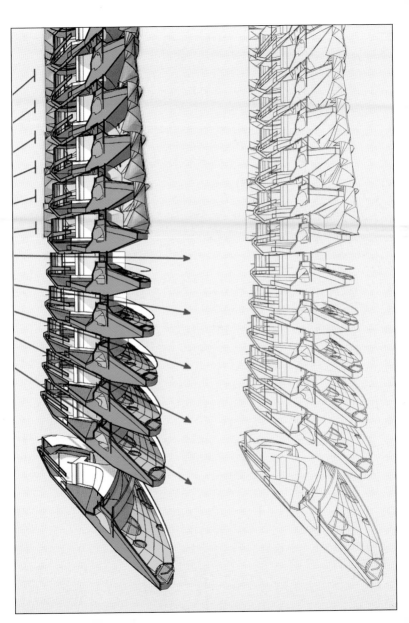

a639c

Ecosystem (RE)Generator

Ricardo Prata	Architect	rp@sala5.net
	EU_Portugal	FAUP, Portugal + ETSAM, Spain

ECOSYSTEM (RE)GENERATOR The main goal of this project was to create a self-sufficient and ecological orientated housing machine that can be used to regenerate ecosystems. It can provide clean energy, produce organic fertilizer, store and purify rain water and still be used as a wildlife stimulator. Due to its strong thermic resistance and to its perfect endurance it can be located outside urban contexts. **ENERGETIC SELF-SUFFICIENT** This energetic self-sufficiency is achieved through a complex system of photovoltaic cellules applied in the main facade of the building and connected to the general electric grid; designed as a geometrical pattern. **SOIL REGENERATOR** The building also disposes a natural mechanism of recycling organic waste through a bio-alchemic garden located in the basement. **WATER COLLECTOR** The principal "fuel" and energetic supplier of the building is the rain water. **WILDLIFE STIMULATOR** This building was also designed to respond positively to the natural environment and to the biological context that surrounds him, in order to become one of the pieces of a larger ecosystem.

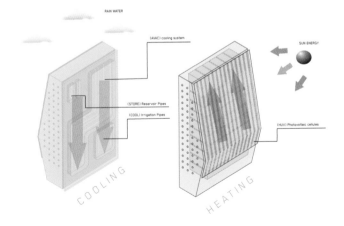

RAIN WATER

(AVAC) cooling system

(STORE) Reservoir Pipes

(COOL) Irrigation Pipes

SUN ENERGY

(HUV) Photovoltaic cellules

COOLING

HEATING

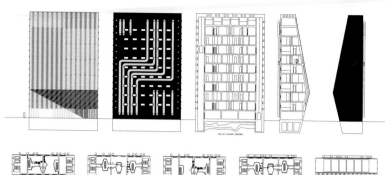

| – Rosa Fraga
– Octavio Tarancón
  Burg | – Architect | – hilvanestudio@gmail.com |
| | – EU_Spain | – Studio Hilvane |

1– **URBAN MODELS** The urban model is the beginning of energetic saving.

2– **SELF-SUFFICIENT COLLECTIVE HOUSING / SOCIAL SUSTAINABLE = URBAN VARIETY** Sustainable is not only energetic saving installations. Energetic saving has to be based on social sustainability. The present urban models create areas where one activity grows without control (congestion in city centre) or create lack of activity areas with dependence on nearby quarters of the city. An area of the city is self-sufficient when it has a variety of activities.

3– **URBAN STRATEGY: DESIGN + PROCESS** Design makes emphasis on dense, collective and complexity of activities structure in order to create complex proceses. This structure enhances communication between people. The energy-saving community installations to become cheaper and realistic.

4– **SELF-SUFFICIENT AND INTERACTIVE** Design is not an autonomous organism. The self-sufficient project is connected to nearby structures in order to balance the excess and the lack of interaction.

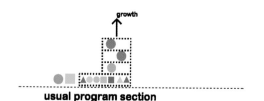

usual program section

proposal program section

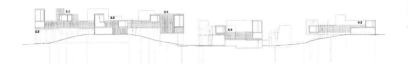

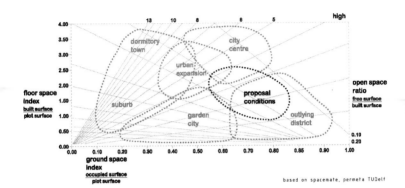

floor space index
built surface
plot surface

ground space index
occupied surface
plot surface

open space ratio
free surface
built surface

based on spacemate, permeta TUDelf

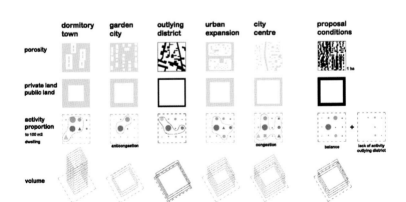

	dormitory town	garden city	outlying district	urban expansion	city centre	proposal conditions
porosity						1 ha
private land public land						
activity proportion to 100 m2 dwelling		anticongestion		congestion		balance + lack of activity outlying district
volume						

PROGRAM

major cultural library museum ▪ bar restaurant ● theater cinema ▲ shop ▲ garage workshop ● market ▪ office ● hotel house ● green space (with sport) ● sport gym ▲ education ● service ▪

| **b5764** | **Cooperative Housing** ⊕ | **CH** |

| –Carolina Galeazzi
–Leticia Teixeira
Rodrigues
–Gustavo Jaquet
Ribeiro | – Architect | – caro_poa@yahoo.com.br |
| | – SA_Brazil | – Federal University of Rio Grande do Sul |

Moving toward social equality is a fundamental issue for sustainable development. In Latin America the lack of housing is a serious problem and requires urgent solutions. The current housing politics do not guarantee credit facilities for the most demanding population. Thus, through organization and union, some communities search the conditions to reach not only the acquisition of an individual house, but also education, qualification and work. The present proposal has, as a central parameter, the participation of the future owners in the process of planning and construction. The organization in independent and self-managing housing cooperative increases the maturity of its integrant, which is responsible for the quality of life improvement of the community.

The construction with earth is part of the Brazilian culture since its origin. The properties of earth constructions indicate an excellent alternative for cooperative housing construction: simplicity of construction, low energy consumption, raw material abundance, minimum waste generation and excellent thermal and acoustic conditions.

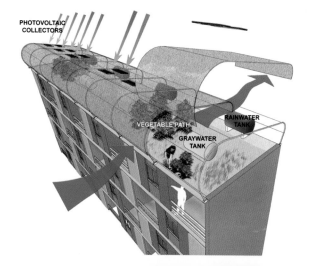

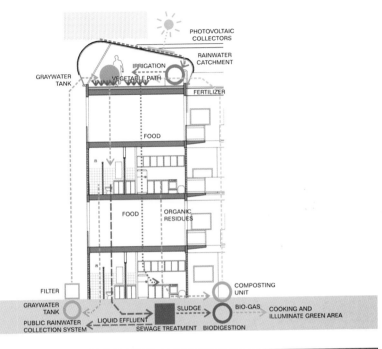

-Israel Paez
-Marcos Zaragoza Cuffí
- Student
- shaggy_paez@hotmail.com

- EU_Spain
- ARKMORRANA

The information developed in this project is a three-scale work: urban metamorphosis, an architectonic model and a conceptual catalog.

"Urban" is understood as a social, cultural and ecological outline necessary to develop a real sustainable metamorphosis. Only with this proliferation of ideas change can occur.

An architectural model, an example of systems applied to the self-sufficiency. A proposal combining ecological systems.

A conceptual catalog of possible schemes of use, gadgets to be incorporated into existing building and hybrid uses that improve the difference between consumption and production.

The the project is located in a degenerated urban tissue undergoing gentrification. There are a lot of opportunity fields, ruined buildings that will become plots to be constructed.

The urban objective is a change in the market inertia to sustainable processes. The strategy is acupuncture where punctual developments will change the overall living outline.

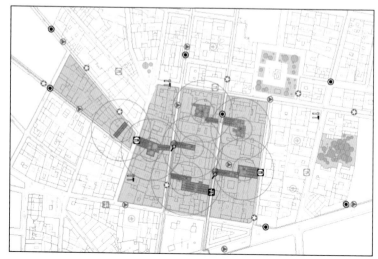

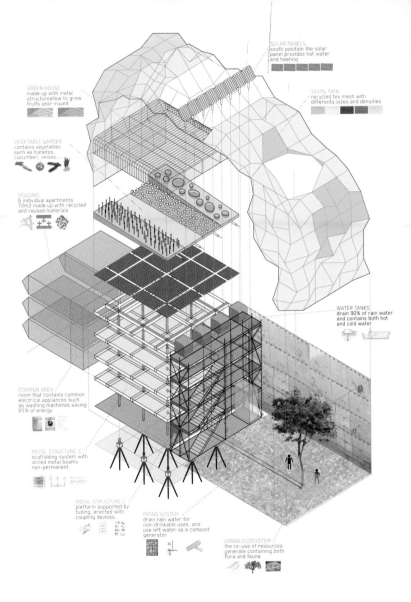

SOLAR PANELS
south position the solar panel provides hot water and heating

GREEN HOUSE
made up with metal structure allow to grow fruits year-round

TEXTIL SKIN
recycled tex mesh with differents sizes and densities

VEGETABLE GARDEN
contains vegetables such as tometos, cucumber, onions...

HOUSING
6 individual apartments 72m2 made up with recycled and reused materials

WATER TANKS
drain 90% of rain water and contains both hot and cold water

COMMON AREA
room that contains common electrical appliances such as washing machines saving 65% of energy

METAL STRUCTURE 1
scaffolding system with drilled metal beams non-permanent

METAL STRUCTURE 2
platform supported by tubing, erected with coupling devices.

PIPING SYSTEM
drain rain water for non-drinkable uses, and use left water as a compost generator

URBAN ECOSYSTEM
the re-use of resources generate containing both flora and fauna

f33a2 Urban Rhizome CH

Jeong-Der Ho Deland Wai-Man Leong	Architect	deland8@yahoo.com
	AS_Taiwan	Architectural Asscociation School of architecture

Due to the complexities in urban conditions, the urban rhizome is devised for tracing and interweaving urban textures based on their operational processing. To deal with the ever changing urban fluxes, instant reactions in various scales are empowered to resonate with the pulses from outside which leads to architecture of responsive volatility. Appropriate technologies are implemented to improve the interaction between the earth and the artificial landscape. **THE TEXTURE MAP** Through the Urban Rhizome, a new resource network is linked. The texture map includes the electricity from fuel cells and plastic solar cells; the water reused from rain for service necessities and building temperature control; the composting from kitchen refuse and garden waste for earth amendment, and its byproduct, methane, from which the fuel cell can extract H_2 as its energy source; the vibration as the energy source for ubiquitous computing to sense the micro-environment shift which helps the building adjust its gesture to the surroundings.

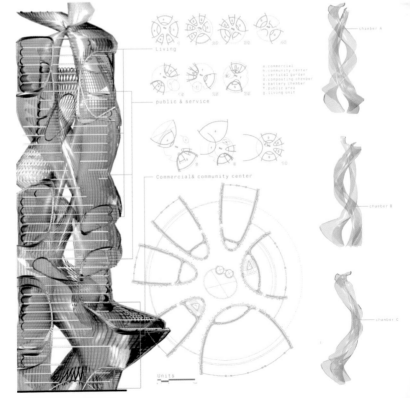

Living

a. commercial
b. community center
c. vertical garden
d. composting chamber
e. battery chamber
f. public area
g. living unit

public & service

Commercial & community center

Units

chamber A

chamber B

chamber C

-Martin Anthony Yong	- Architect	- martin.yong@alumni.rca.ac.uk
-Manfred Yuen		
-Sally Quinn	- EU_UK	- Royal College of Art, UK

"Vertical Communities" embraces the idea of self-sustaining ecosystems found in nature. Living, working and commuting populations within Hong Kong, each with their own sets of behaviors, interact, exploiting the problems of one to symbiotically benefit all.

Using the core of a skyscraper as a chimney, differences in pressure and temperature between the subterranean and top are harnessed to provide passive air-conditioning. These currents are also used to generate energy. The chimney also ventilates the hot subway environment.

Vertical cores, filled with naturally filtering sand and rock, feed grey water into reservoirs. The water is treated and stored for local use.

Linking the potential of one system with that of another, a mutually beneficial "eco-system" is created. The subway, street and home all benefit from this symbiosis. The physical and symbolic core of the building is visible and celebrated.

─Erez Amitay ─Fioraso Francesca	─ Architect	─ eramitay@yahoo.com
	─ AS_Israel	─ IUAV, Venezia

The project aims to create a residential area in the old port of Jaffa, Tel-Aviv. The structure is entirely based on a system of 'dry' assembly, which considers the possible dismantling of the constructions at the end of their "life-cycle" and the re-use of the building materials.

The kasbah-like layout of the houses allows the air to circulate through the openings between the flats, improving the ventilation and the cooling of the structure. The south and west facades are covered by deciduous climbing plants that absorb solar radiation in summer, but allow light to penetrate during the winter. The open green spaces act as wind corridors that channel the constant sea breeze into the buildings. The irrigation of large green spaces is sustained by a constructed wetland system that naturally recycles the waste water through the use of plants and micro-organisms. This way the whole area acts as one balanced and autonomous organism.

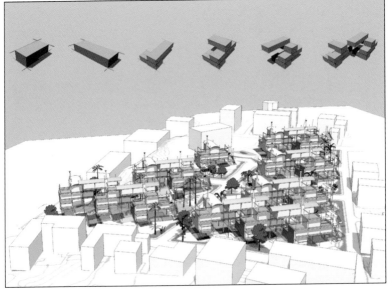

0e724 Hybrid Tower

- Esther Rovira
- Josep Maria Guito
- Ruben Ferez
- Maria Campos

- Architect

- estherrovira@coac.es

- EU_Spain

- UIC, Barcelona

The proposal is an endless tower that takes profit of the building's structure and gravity to produce effective recycling processes to generate the needed resources to live within today's quality standards. The system is based on three simple devices: service towers – square meters – activity boxes. Four Service towers provide the needed resources taking them from precipitation and wind; transforming them by using recycling processes which are developed along the height of the building within the building's structure: climate service – energy service – communication service – recycle service. All together make possible the self-sufficient system. One of the advantages is that being an endless system, the tower can grow in high to update to new demands of housing. Another advantage is that the facade can mutate depending on the site's environment, remaining the indoor skin in glass and being the outdoor skin different.

service towers

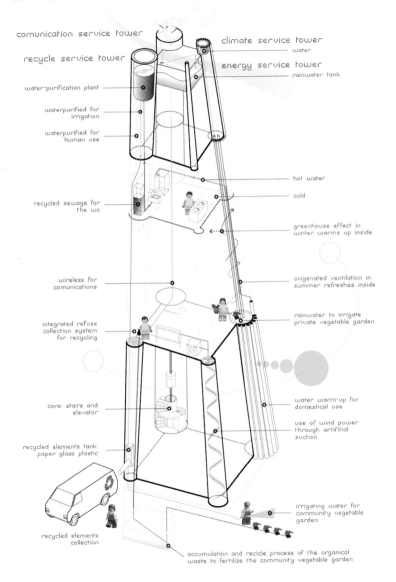

comunication service tower

climate service tower
water

recycle service tower

energy service tower
rainwater tank

water-purification plant

waterpurified for irrigation

waterpurified for human use

recycled sewage for the wc

hot water

cold

greenhouse effect in winter warms up inside

wireless for comunications

oxigenated ventilation in summer refreshes inside

integrated refuse collection system for recycling

rainwater to irrigate private vegetable garden

core: stairs and elevator

water warm-up for domestical use

use of wind power through artifitial suction

recycled elements tank: paper glass plastic

recycled elements collection

irrigating water for community vegetable garden

accumulation and recicle process of the organical waste to fertilize the community vegetable garden

4327e Housing in Montreal CH

| Godefroy Meyer | Architect | vonmeyer@hotmail.com |
| | EU_France | Université de Montreal |

MONTREAL / DOWNTOWN AREA / CANADA Through form and material, the south wall acquires multiple properties. In order to protect dwelling spaces from a direct contact with exterior air conditions, the wall is double skinned. The latter's material composition is of concrete. The combination of form/matter acts simultaneously as an air temperature moderator and heat absorber. The wall's inner cavity acts as insulation. Solar panels are favorably angled to receive an important amount of light, thus providing a percentage of the energy requirements of the building. The presence of the slope also allows for water collection. Heat gathered from the thermal mass offered by the wall's mineral composition is transferred to the reservoir, in turn heating the water. The north, east and west walls soften the south wall's strong identity. Composed of an horizontal wood lattice, the former is a potential support for the growth of vegetation such as ivy or vines.

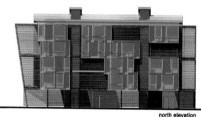

west elevation   north elevation

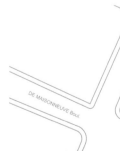
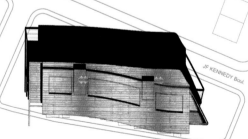

DE MAISONNEUVE Boul.

JF KENNEDY Boul.

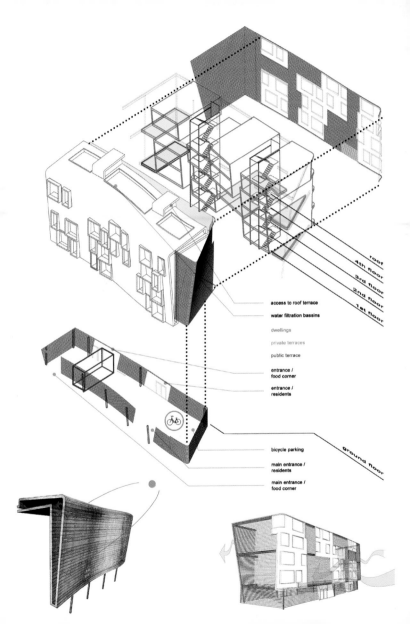

access to roof terrace

water filtration bassins

dwellings

private terraces

public terrace

entrance /
food corner

entrance /
residents

bicycle parking

main entrance /
residents

main entrance /
food corner

roof

4th floor

3rd floor

2nd floor

1st floor

ground floor

d18f5	**Zoom-House**		**CH**

–Marco Scarpinato –Vincenzo Guagliardo	– Architect	– www.autonomeforme.it – info@autonomeforme.it
–Lorenza Majorana –Lucia Pierro –Carmelo Vitrano	– EU_Italy	– Autonome forme

The project is proposed for Bhopal, India, a site of heavy chemical contamination. It proposes the integration of the future technologies of ambient regeneration. The self-sufficient collective housing is situated on the polluted site, in two stages:

1- Phytodepuration: Choose a point. It activates the purifying function. The water is purified by the plants and it is collected in a basin.

2- Construction: In according to the context and social-economic demaind of the community; defines the building density, generating the different volumes of the houses.

The dimensional articulation works like a zoom in/out that defines the versions of the houses generating the different configurations. The prototype's ability for adaption guarantees its sustainability and its ability of maintenance, integrating all the functions for ambient comfort and for energetic auto-sufficiency.

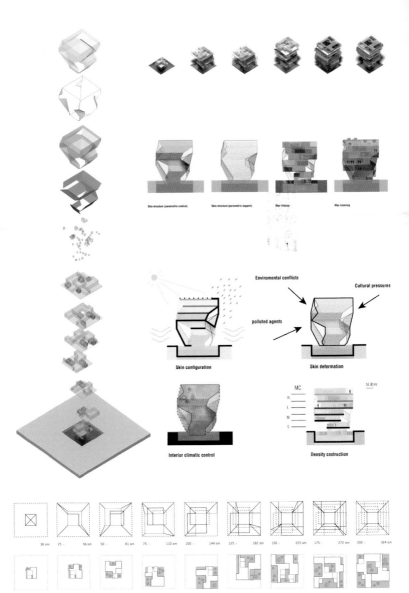

Skin structure (parametric control)   Skin structure (parametric support)   Max Volume   Max covering

Enviromental conflicts

Cultural pressures

polluted agents

Skin configuration

Skin deformation

Interior climatic control

Density costruction

MC

16.00 mr

1 _ floor _ 25 green _ 75 house   2 _ floor _ 30 green _ 70 house   3 _ floor _ 35 green _ 65 house   4 _ floor _ 40 green _ 60 house   5 _ floor _ 55 green _ 45 house   6 _ floor _ 50 green _ 50 house   7 _ floor _ 60 green _ 40 house   8 _ floor _ 65 green _ 35 house   9 _ floor _ 70 green _ 30 house

eS600 | Regenerating Hubs | CH

–Jonathan Arnabat –Jaume Canals	– Architect	– jonathanarnabat@yahoo.es
	– EU_Spain	

Within a well known area in the heart of Barcelona, the Eixample Quarter, we propose a series of Regenerating Hubs, a real 'machine' for living, breathing, producing energy, recycling the huge quantity of man-made waste, and for managing scarce resources, such as water. A green lung, a pollution sponge, a building that is self-sufficient, not only from the technological perspective but also from a social, economic and cultural point of view. The building is structured along a great vertebral column, containing a communication center and access areas. In addition, five ecological and self-sufficient infrastructures are planned to take care of energy and material resource management. **SOLAR STRUCTURE** Collecting solar radiation through photovoltaic panels. **RECYCLING STRUCTURES** Ducts for glass, aluminum, plastic, paper and organic waste. Collection of dust pollution, heavy particles in suspension, through an electrically charged structure. The collection of the telecommunication waves would be focused in a single point in the block: Telephone, Internet, TV, radio, etc. **GREEN STRUCTURE** Each living space has a landscaped roof for home-grown cultivation of vegetables, plants and small trees and a lateral green house.

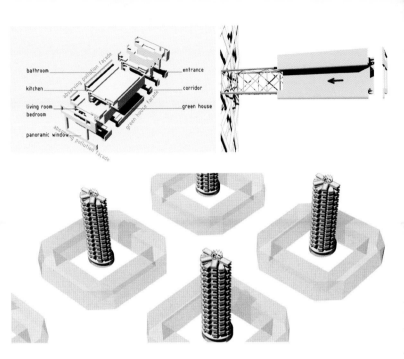

bathroom

kitchen

living room
bedroom

panoramic window

absorbing pollution facade

green house facade

entrance

corridor

green house

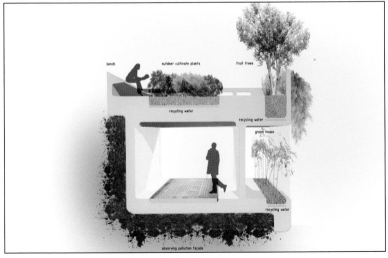

bench   outdoor cultivate plants   fruit trees

recycling water

recycling water

green house

recycling water

absorbing pollution facade

- Pedro Henrique Morais
- Antônio do Prado Valladares Andrade

- Architect

- SA_Brazil

- pedromorais.arquiteto@gmail.com

- Universidade Federal de Minas Gerais, Brazil

THE SUBJECT Almost three million people live in Belo Horizonte, the third largest metropolis in Brazil. In 1951, Brazil is in a "welfare state" and progress/technology agenda is in the air. The plan: a huge building, with 1067 units of different typologies. Former state governor, Juscelino Kubitscheck's idea was to build, by the hands of Oscar Niemeyer, the "Brazilian Eiffel Tower". If these buildings keep wasting so much natural resources the question will not have been solved. This proposal is an attempt to think local, opening ways for global action.

THE PROJECT Intervention strategies are focused on four major points:

1- Energy self-sufficiency through the use of Photovoltaic Silicon Panels and Solar Water Heating Panels.

2- Water saving system works the collection of rainwater from roofs, gravity triple-filtering it and pumping it back up for reuse. (Excluding drinking and cooking.)

3- Easy waste separation and recycling, through use of the existing chute and a mechanical separator.

4- Introduction of organic mass in vacant areas to promote thermal comfort and air quality combined with common facilities.

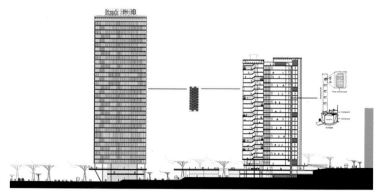

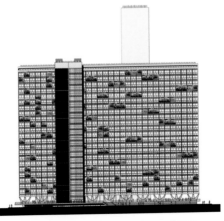

83a3c Ecosystem Injections CH

1st Prize Collective Housing

- Daniel Ibañez Moreno
- Rodrigo Rubio Cuadrado
- Alberto Alvarez Agea

- Architect

- EU_Spain

- danielibanezmoreno@hotmail.com

- ETSAM, Madrid

1– CHOOSING AN ENVIRONMENT BECAUSE OF ITS MAXIMUM SOCIAL, CULTURAL AND ENERGETIC INTENSITY → ALGIERS This location presents significant conditions based on the ecological point of view, seeing that social, cultural, geographic and energetic factors intervene and connect.

2– INSERTING THREE ARTIFICIAL ECOSYSTEMs IN THE CITY AS A GLOBAL PROJECT STRATEGY This strategy tries inserting three artificial ecosystems in order to provide answers to the ecological needs of the city, in three different, characteristic sites: CITY AREA-TERRAIN VAGUE–PORT AREA. We decided to insert an ad hoc ecosystem in each of these three plots: CITY AREA → LAURISILVA ecosystem, presents a high level of humidity and fresh green spaces with high plant density. Trees form a dense, diverse woodland. TERRAIN VAGUE → FRUIT ecosystem, presents medium density in the landscape, with low-key trees and a blanket of flowers beneath. It's a very colorful clear-structured ecosystem with aligned spaces, neatly positioned. PORT AREA → SOMIEDO ecosystem, presents low density in the landscape, marked by green undulating hills with pedestrian paths. It brings low temperatures and a high level of humidity. Having these landscape objectives in mind, we artificially insert them in the city.

3– ARCHITECTURAL DEVELOPMENT. GENERATING HYBRID-ECOLOGICAL TOWERS The nodes work in a web. Each one specializes in a specific energy generating process, depending on the surrounding conditions. So, a tower with high reception ability will emit energy to another tower, which specialises in storage, in exchange for parking spaces (for example). In each location specific percentages of reception, recycling and storage are obtained. So, node 03 will have 10% storage, 60% recycling and 30% reception. The facade configuration depends directly on these percentages. How it is organized in the cross section (below, in the middle, above) is dictated by the functioning interests of each ecological module. Apart from this, each ecological module houses the different programs, regardless of what kind of module it might be: housing, public program, green areas and non-programmed space. Modules and programs are wrapped with a conditioning-artificial skin, which rehabilitates the character of the insertion ecosystem.

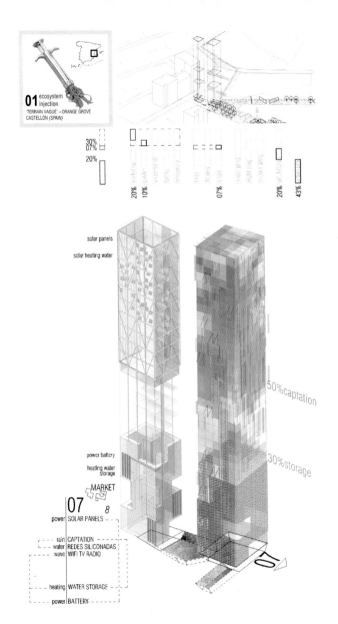

01 ecosystem injection

'TERRAIN VAGUE' > ORANGE GROVE
CASTELLÓN *(SPAIN)*

30%
07%
20%

20% working
10% trade
ss-prof-al
family
tertiary-l
07% fires
ficens
crops
fish food
night prod.
other prod.
20% air Mbps
43%

solar panels
solar heating water

50%captation

30%storage

power battery
heating water
storage

MARKET

07 8

power SOLAR PANELS

rain CAPTATION
water REDES SILICONADAS
wave WIFI TV RADIO

heating WATER STORAGE

power BATTERY

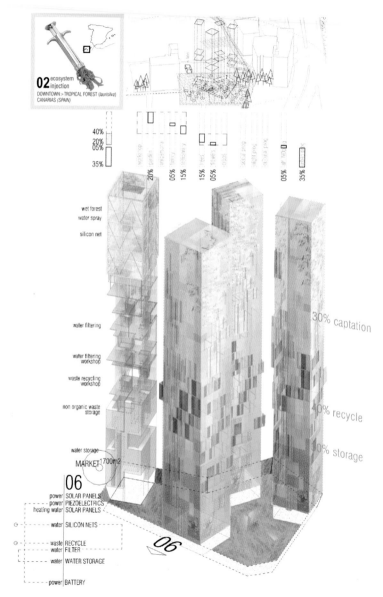

02 ecosystem injection
DOWNTOWN > TROPICAL FOREST (laurisilva)
CANARIAS (SPAIN)

40%
20%
05%
35%

20%   05%   15%   15%   05%   05%   35%

workshop
garden
greenhouse
library
laboratory
spa
rest
towers
pool
social prog
night prog
acqua prog
air prog
services

wet forest
water spray

silicon net

30% captation

water filtering

water filtering
workshop

waste recycling
workshop

40% recycle

non organic waste
storage

30% storage

water storage

MARKET 1700m2

06

power   SOLAR PANELS
power   PIEZOELECTRICS
heating water SOLAR PANELS

water   SILICON NETS

waste   RECYCLE
water   FILTER

water   WATER STORAGE

power   BATTERY

06

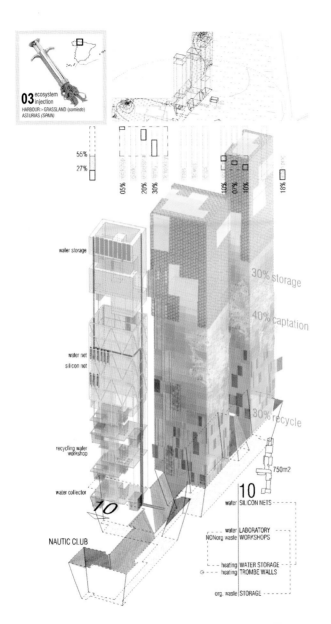

03 ecosystem injection
HARBOUR>GRASSLAND (somiedo)
ASTURIAS (SPAIN)

55%
27%

05%   20%   30%   10%   0%   10%   18%

water storage

30% storage

40% captation

water net
silicon net

30% recycle

recycling water
workshop

750m2

water collector

10

10

water SILICON NETS

water LABORATORY
NONorg waste WORKSHOPS

heating WATER STORAGE
heating TROMBE WALLS

NAUTIC CLUB

org. waste STORAGE

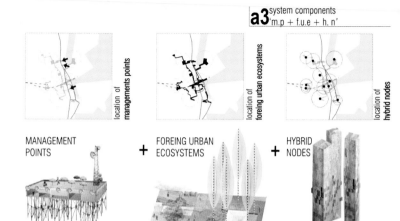

MANAGEMENT POINTS + FOREING URBAN ECOSYSTEMS + HYBRID NODES

THE IMPERATIVE COMPONENTS OF THESE ARTIFICIAL ECOSYSTEMS ARE:
1. Several 'management points' which create the scenery, as well as organise develop and mantain each of the three landscapes.
2. Artificial 'rug' which contains within all the elements of energetic exchange and contribution, green elements and public programs.
3. Vertical 'nodes' (towers) each one made out of the sum of three ecological modules: reception, recycling, storage. Each one becomes a constructive type, which adds up to the rest creating these towers.

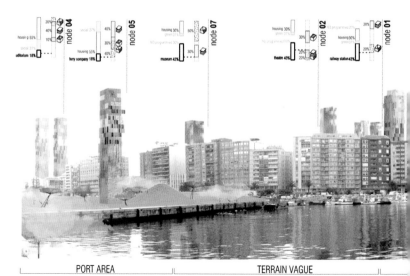

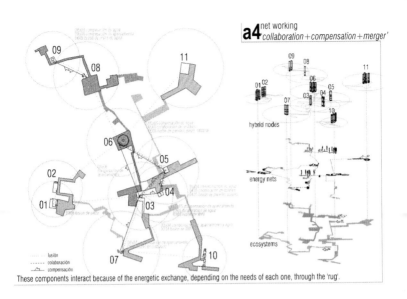

hybrid nodes

energy nets

ecosystems

lusión
colaboración
compensación

These components interact because of the energetic exchange, depending on the needs of each one, through the 'rug'.

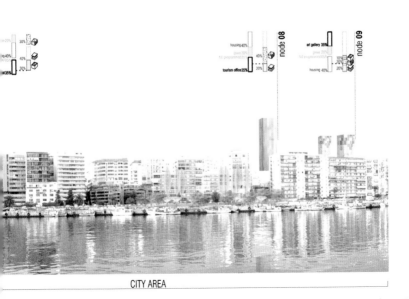

node 08

housing 40%
green 20%
h5 equipment 20%
tourism office 35%

node 09

art gallery 35%
green 20%
h5 equipment 20%
housing 40%

CITY AREA

5

Modulated and Coast

This is the most frequently used self-sufficient housing production system of the taxonomy. The dwelling—the module—is conceived as a self-sufficient unit, as a part made by mass production systems, that is manufactured as a model, fundamentally to be used in association with other parts of the same kind. It is this unit, at once constituted and closed, that observes the closest relation between surface and volume and pays most attention to production costs since mass production, too, essentially optimizes resources and means. The interior of Modulated and Cost is more neutral and often indeterminate, since it houses activity rather than generating it within, containing it in this host dwelling with an interior unmarked by definitive codes and allowing occupiers to freely appropriate the total volume and enjoy the space by means of objects introduced without contextualization into this impartial interior. The module may be sited in a variety of residual or other locations, since its very nature means that it can be piled up, recomposed and rearranged according to the individual setting.

There are various alternatives. As part of a larger association of the module, [config], it is arranged according to its integration into larger infrastructures and reconfigures interior spaces in keeping with the modification of its facings, thereby improving isolation and energy behaviour while attending to the economic impact of production.

More autonomous, solitary elements are Minimum mobile module and Mo cab, simpler standard units that vary the composition and adaptation of their constituent panels according to their orientation.

Habitation unit type A, like a box containing other boxes, unfolds a series of containers for various uses and arrangements.

Worthy of particular mention is the conceptual approach of the Committee 123 module (second place in the Self-Sufficient Single Housing Contest), which makes the most of the low-tech characteristics of the context in which it is set, often a peripheral place marked by social and economic marginalization.

It offers solutions to water and oxygen supplies and thermal regulation, as well as managing waste and producing some of its resources, with constant attention to the costs and feasibility of production.

02a84 Bio-Fold

SH

| Julio Ferrer Piñeiro | Student | julione@hotmail.com |
| Maria Graciela Soto Fuenmayor | SA_Venezuela | Universidad del Zulia |

Speaking about the Earth in a general way, we refer to the planet, which is a resource container of natural elements and the place we inhabit.

That's the meaning of the Bio-Fold; a part of the soil or space of the earth that rises and folds to create a habitat; earthly, it has all the elements needed to allow for everyday life, almost completely and autonomously. These elements are represented by systems. For its continuous operation the house needs: water, electricity, sewage, gas, light. Its inhabitants' needs are within the fold, which acts as a sustaining core. This earth-fold is an element container. In this case it is a fold that seeks autonomy, producing and using resources rationally. Therefore, it is more aware and sensitive about the environment, using alternative ways of energy.

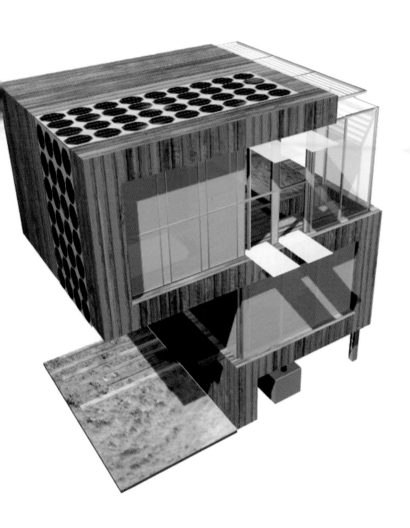

| Emil Ivanescu | Architect | emmmil52000@yahoo.com |
| | EU_Romania | Ion Mincu University of Architecture & Urbanism |

The site, Belgium, in the Fagnes Forest. We obtained a hybrid concept of a fountain and a protected sleeping place. This hybrid object will become a sign of the forests not only by design but also by the complex facilities which integrate the object with nature and with the tourist paths.

A description includes: a wooden deck with a drinking fountain and the exhibition of a regional map with a history of place, a water collection and purification system, an electrical generating system, and a sleeping layer. The structure is metal and the walls are sandwich panels, wood and technical membranes.

The skin could assume different colors, motifs, decorations. In the end, we have an object that could express the site context, but, also which could be a standard piece of architecture that finds its place both in nature and in an urbanized area: an information box, a public fountain, a place to sleep.

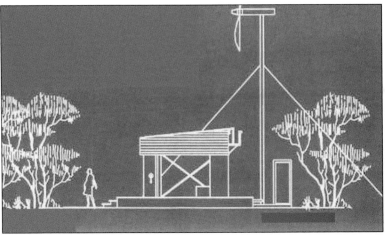

7e885	Adaptability		5H

| Nathan John Williams | Architect | nathan@designtothink.com | |
| | NA_USA | Oklahoma State University | |

Using water, sun and wind a series of components can be created and plugged-in to bring the home to life. This "plug and play" theory allows the home to "adapt" itself to its location and to the family. Windows are punched in to create shading and reduce direct light. It also creates a light shelf that bounces light deeper into the home. Stairs: which serve as the vertical circulation for people, also act as the vertical circulation for ventilation, where ceilings are angled to force rising hot air towards the stairs for ventilation. Panels: photovoltaic cells can be combined with the solar collectors to create the energy needed to power the home. These panels also act as rain collectors. The blade: harnesses wind and updrafts that produces energy. The windmills can also be unplugged to add more surface area for solar collectors or photovoltaic cells.

7f314 ECOstrategy house SH

- Eitaro Hirota
- Sengsack Tsoi
- Keith Ng
- Tomoyuki Shimizu
- Tsukasa Takenaka
- Aya Okabe

- Architect

- oratorih@hotmail.com

- NA_Canada

- S.A. Studio limited

ECOstrategy (Es) House is not self sufficient. The product emerges not as a something unique to a specific image but is the result of the manipulation of a system or strategy. Es House presents itself as an alternative to mass produced market housing, with the economy suitable to the mass market, not by the standardization of form, but with a focus on proficiency and adaptability. The organization of Es House diverges from the prescriptive organization of the plan to zones characterized by their properties.

The smart composition of the zones allows Es House to respond to various sites, climates, user cultures, and most importantly, it offers a strategy to accommodate change and evolution.

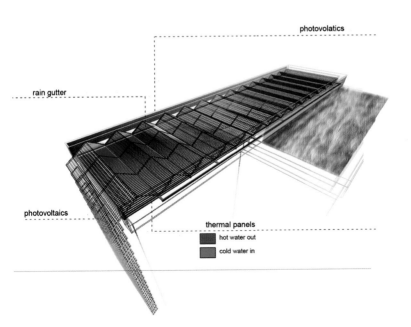

photovolatics

rain gutter

photovoltaics

thermal panels

hot water out

cold water in

8ce48	Minimum Mobile Module	5H

| Flavio Galvagni | Architect | avio@lab-zero.com |
| | EU_Italy | Lab Zero |

The "Minimum Mobile Module" is designed as a fully equipped living unit that is the size of a 20' shipping container, transportable by standard truck or helicopter, adapting to a wide variety of social, cultural and site conditions. It is provided with adjustable legs, retractible rooms, large windows (to ensure high natural illumination levels and exterior views), and four modules that contain a shower, a wc, a kitchen and an air conditioning system. Currently, the transitory form of architecture proposes a less violent and stable relationship with the landscape, be it built or unbuilt, thereby renouncing possession and domination of the host environment.

The module can be inserted anywhere, without appropriating, finishing or consuming local resources. Two, large folding solar panels satisfy the required amount electricity consumption and act as passive rain collectors. An integrated waste system provides total autonomy. When fully unfolded, the proposal doubles its minimum floor area (from 15 to 30 m²), easily activated by two people in a few hours and suitable for inhabitation by a maximum of three persons.

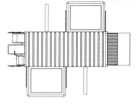

Close mode

Active mode

Plan layout

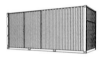

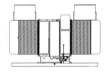

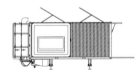

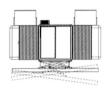

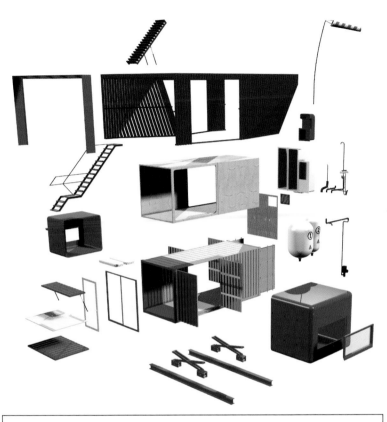

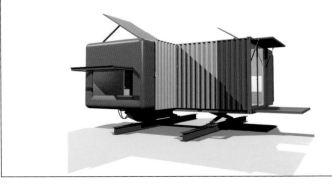

| Fiona Nixon | Archi- | fionanixon@minifienixon.com |
| | AC_Australia | Minifie Nixon |

A stone home is a modularized house design for use in a new suburb in a disused basalt quarry in Melbourne's inner suburbs. Multiple configurations of the stone home, suiting a range of site orientations and family structures, may be assembled from standardized functional and formal parts.

The embodied energy of the stone home is reduced by salvaging material from site excavation for use in wall construction and as concrete aggregate. Timber framing sourced from CO_2 sequestering plantations is used for internal walls, the upper floor and roof. Harvested storm and grey water is stored in an outdoor pool that employs evaporation to cool the house. Solar heating and a greenhouse on the house's northern side warm the interior in winter. The aesthetics of the home allude to the volcanic history of the site; igneous rock used in the massive base and bounding walls, vitrified materials-glass and ceramic tiles, providing enclosure and finishes.

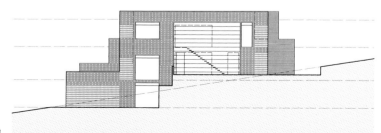

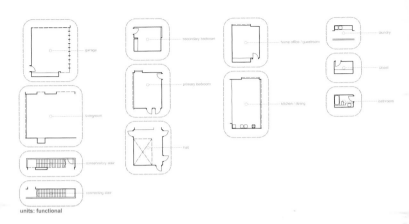

garage

secondary bedroom

home office / guestroom

laundry

living room

primary bedroom

kitchen / dining

closet

conservatory stair

hall

bathroom

connecting stair

units: functional

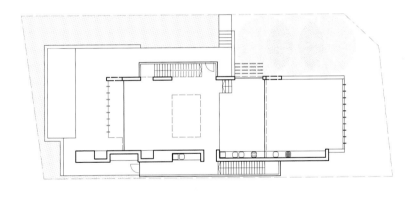

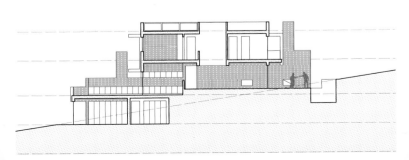

| – Emilios Michael | – Architect | – www.imarch.net
– aimilios@imarch.net |
| | – EU_Greece | – National Technical University of Athens |

The unit is intended to cover the housing needs emerging during and after political unrest, war encounters, or natural disasters. Though the proposed unit is a preliminary shelter, helping to eliminate the use of tents, it is qualitatively adequate and spatially efficient for use over a prolonged time period. The entire proposal is characterized by a principle of economy in both construction and architectural design, respecting spatial substance as well as operating and manufacturing costs.

Minimization of a settlement's energy needs is pursued via optimal exploitation of a passive energy design and employment of advanced technology systems that exploit solar energy.

The potential of addressing a range of housing needs, determined by each family's size and composition, is investigated through the modification, expandability, and transformation of the exterior unit shell and the internal equipment of each shelter.

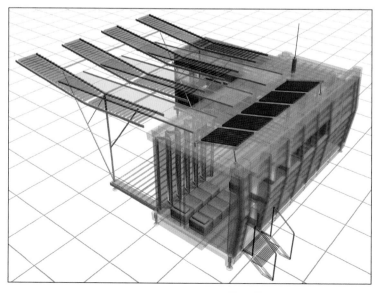

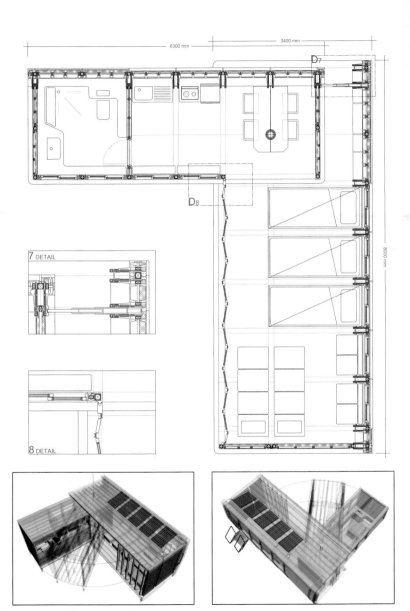

6300 mm

3400 mm

D7

8000 mm

7 DETAIL

D8

8 DETAIL

134c6 Movable Home

SH

Sonja Tinney
Silke Henning

Architect — sonjatinney@gmx.de

EU_Germany — Universität Hannover

Flexibility and mobility play a large role in modern living. We travel constantly and need more and more places for short-term stays. Normally one travels by plane or car, searching for accommodationg in a neighboring city. Every city has an idle industrial railway system.

These unused systems were the basis of our work. We created a moveable home which drives on rails like a wagon and uses these idle networks to stay within the city. The moveable home has external dimensions of 3.50m and contains all necessary components for daily life. The wagon can be driven out on the size of 16 square meters. In the interior various elements can be folded out the walls and the floor. Also in terms of power supply, water and heating, the moveable home is independent and flexible. The necessary equipment is placed on the roof or in the double floor, easily sustaining operations for up to three days.

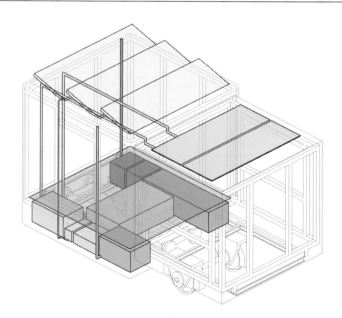

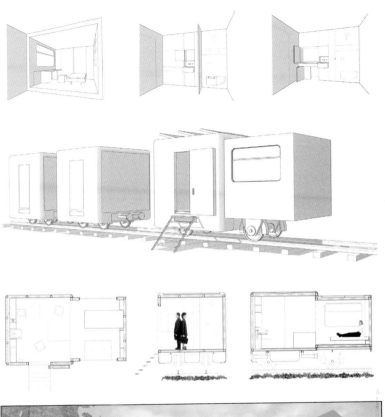

| Samuel Tan | Architect | sam_in_aust@hotmail.com |
| | AC_Australia | University of Western Australia |

We propose the following three keys points, essential for the making of self-sufficient, collective houses, by considering their energy, food and water needs for domestic comfort, as well as flexibility for the changing demographic and social changes of the occupants.

1– RECYCLING BIO WASTE TO PRODUCE ENERGY AND FOOD Transforming our bio waste in stages from liquefaction, carbon, to nitrogen transformation. In this process, we can also obtain natural gasses, a source of energy for our domestic lives.

2– WATER AND ENERGY EFFICIENT SHELTER AND HOUSING ARRANGEMENT Spatial proportion in relation to sun orientation, as well as over-shadowing in summer, to wind cooling in summer and thermal solar heating in winter. Collecting and storing filtered rainwater in the northern walls, so that it is readily available for drinking, washing, and showering.

3– CHANGING LIFESTYLE PATTERNS AND SIZE If walls are flexible enough to be movable, we can have the possibility of changing layouts by simply pushing, sliding and attaching. Services can be constantly reconfigured and inserted into the helves boxes to be attached into the plug-in service wall.

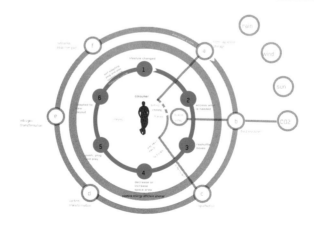

Self sufficient cycle 3
Changing lifestyles patterns and size

DIY flexible shelves boxes **variations**

1   2   3   4   5   6

Plug and play system

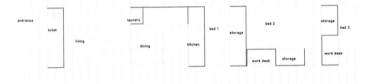

entrance

toilet

living

laundry

dining

kitchen

bed 1

storage

bed 2

storage

work desk   storage

storage

bed 3

work desk

N

dad 38   mum 35   daughter 7   grandmum 68

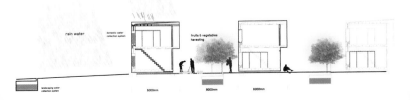

rain water

domestic water
collection system

fruits & vegetables
harvesting

landscaping water
collection system

6000mm   8000mm   6000mm

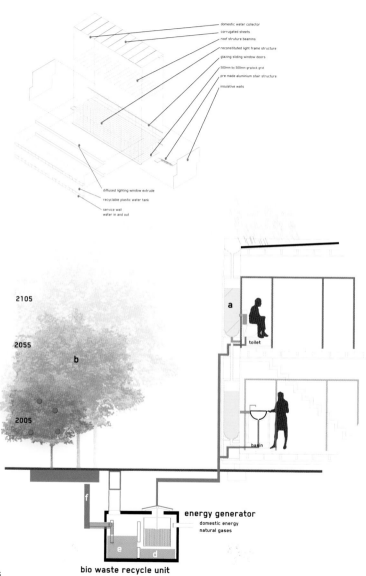

domestic water collector
corrugated sheets
roof struture beamns
reconstituted light frame structure
glazing sliding window doors
500mm by 500mm graplock grid
pre made aluminium stair structure
insulative walls

diffused lighting window extrude
recyclable plastic water tank
service wall
water in and out

2105

2055

b

2005

a

toilet

basin

f

energy generator
domestic energy
natural gases

e   d

bio waste recycle unit

196

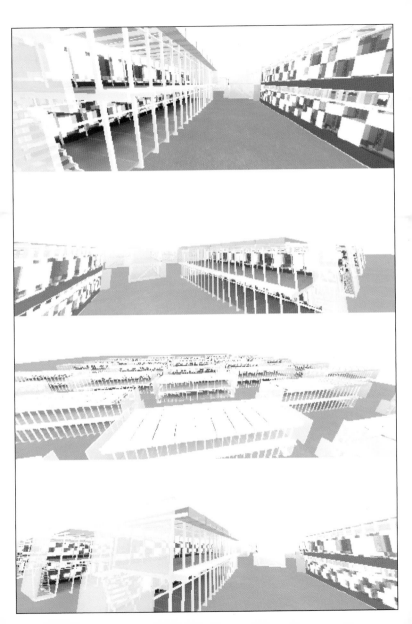

Adelaide Dawn	Architect	adelaidedawn@archcappella.com
	NA _USA	University of Cincinnati

I watched her as she pointed out the window. "See that empty plot over there, I used to have a home on it." My eyes followed her gaze to one of the many holes in the tight grid of the old river town where more than ten years after the devastating 1993 Mississippi floods, abandoned properties looked like so many missing teeth in a sad smile.

The home is an individual's physiological and psychological stand against the elements, and for as long as humanity has set itself apart from nature, natural disasters have defeated this stand. Where better to explore the potential within seeming contradictions of dwelling and dynamic natural forces, than where disaster victims must find peace and healing within the architecture of a world in flux?

What follows is not a design solution for a frozen frame of referenced time, but a time-sensitive equation to reconcile events of the past, traumas of the present, and potentials of the future.

| Paolo Marisco | Architect | paablo@libero.it |
| | EU_Italy | UNICAL |

MOCAB: MOVING CABIN, Mocab's philosophy: small, mobile, flexible, environmently respectful. Mocab768 is a modular dwelling system that adapts to a variety of environments and offers flexible space partitions. The cabin can be set anywhere: in a urban or suburban or rural environment, in single and/or multiple configuration, making use of sustainable buildings materials and using the sun as an alternative energy source.

Built on a 2.98m square grid, mocab768 can be easily transported by truck, and erected on-site by mobile crane. Both inner and outer opaque space partitions are made with composite panels that guarantee sound proofing, thermal insulating and excellent mechanical properties. Transparent, polycarbonate sandwich walls and steel-frame, dynamic shutters complete the cabin. The prefabricated approach does not preclude individual expression: the customer can select different layouts and fittings, creating the ultimate in flexible working and living, making relocation or expansion 'as quick and uncomplicated as possible'.

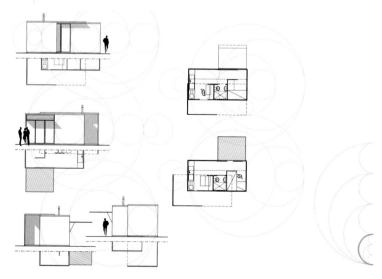

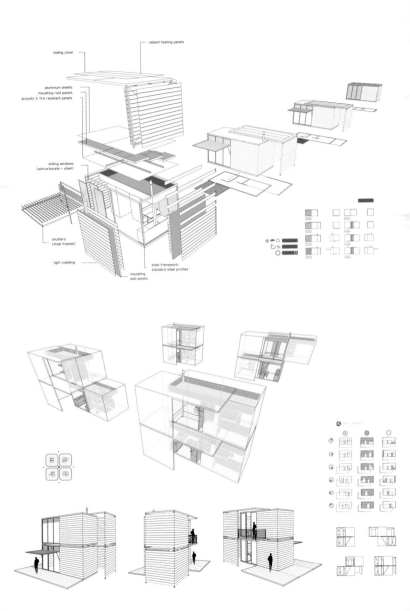

radiant heating panels

sliding cover

aluminium sheets
insulating roof panels
acoustic & fire resistant panels

sliding windows
(polcarbonate + steel)

shutters
(steel framed)

light cladding

insulating
wall panels

steel framework:
standard steel profiles

| **b74ef** | **Movable Home** | | **SH** |

- Natalia Triana
- Juan Carlos Bohorquez

- Architect
- SA_Colombia

- nataliatrianam@yahoo.com
- Universidad de los Andes

Due to its geographic location, Colombia is a country with a lot of privileges, along with a unique producer of tropical woods, not very common around the world (fibers, bamboos, etc.). Currently, there is a misuse of these natural resources. They don't play an important role in the economies of the regions where they are produced. Therefore, our responsibility as architects is to propose new projects that permit these forgotten communities to create a sustainable social, economic and environmental scenario. This architectural posture will create a dramatic change in the national reality.

We propose a new home that is integrated with its surroundings and causes a small environmental impact.

The first stage will be a lot: 9 x 11 m, a unit of progressive dwelling will be conceived from a cubic space that will be supplied by an auto-sustainable system complemented by a traditional system. This unit will be composed by three fringes: A— Auto sustainable services; B— Multifunctional (media room and the chambers); C— Orchard.

FUNCTION SCHEME

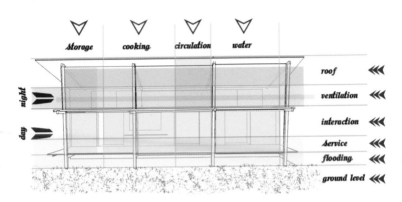

Storage — cooking — circulation — water

roof ◀◀◀
ventilation ◀◀◀
interaction ◀◀◀
service ◀◀◀
flooding ◀◀◀
ground level ◀◀◀

night / day

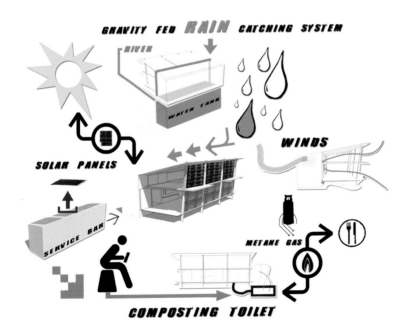

GRAVITY FED **RAIN** CATCHING SYSTEM

RIVER

WATER TANK

SOLAR PANELS

WINDS

SERVICE BAR

METANE GAS

COMPOSTING TOILET

bbd40 Villamelilla

SH

Esteban Varela Fernandez Martin Delgado Nicolás Barriola	Architect	esteban.varela@gmail.com
	SA_Uruguay	Varela+Delgado+Barriola architects

THERMAL EFFICIENCY Folded surface. Maximum exposure to sun-radiation on east, west and north façade to benefit from maximum sunshine. Buffer 1: Concentration of service rooms and circulation area on south side to reduce energy loss. Buffer 2: Transparent envelope that assures the retention of heat through greenhouse effect. Tilted roof: Inclination for maximum energy acquirement on solar water heaters and solar panels. Windows: Various automatic ventilation mechanisms allow temperature regulation according to weather conditions and comfort requirements.

RESOURCES AND WASTE MANAGEMENT Energy: sun-panels + biodigestor + solar water heaters. Water, main uses: purified subterranean water pumped by windmill; water, toilet: collected rain water supplemented by a subterranean source. Food: Partial supply from cultivated land and cattle. Wastewater: controlled disposal and treatment in the constructed wetland. Waste,organic: selection to feed animals and produce bio-compost; waste, inorganic: Collected separately for disposal at recycling centres.

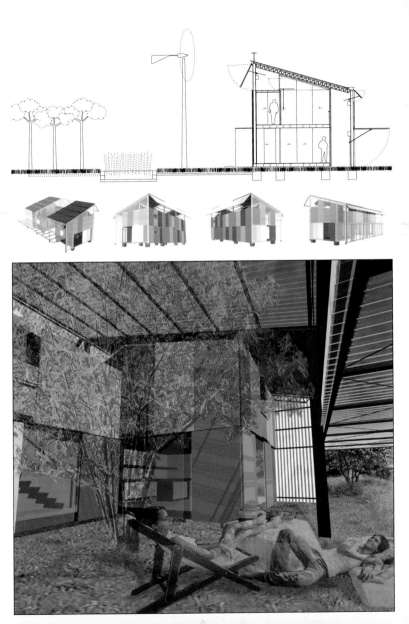

d337e Elrurallof SH

- Sergio Aldama
- Alvaro Moreno
- Horacio Perez Zamora
- Diego Flores

- Student

- SA_Uruguay

- www.nbarchi.com
- balconada@gmail.com

- Balconada

...to rebuild a possible landscape on this forgotten territory, with a house that understands the landscape as own and not as a scenery...

We intend to create an inverse of that offer, a house that is understood as a microclimate, where we asked ourselves about how we would live in such a space. This offer, Elrurallof, contains a microclimate in a single space that suits the house. A space placed over the house, as a rucksack, it accommodates the body it serves.

A microclimate above and house below, with two analogous spaces, winter-summer interchangeable according to its orientation. To concentrate the house into a single space and then open it, expand it, and mix it with the landscape. To think about superimposing processed materials in order to save, use and recycle energy and waste.

A tent with nature inside, a family space at ground-level, a wild space above where the family enjoys the landscape...

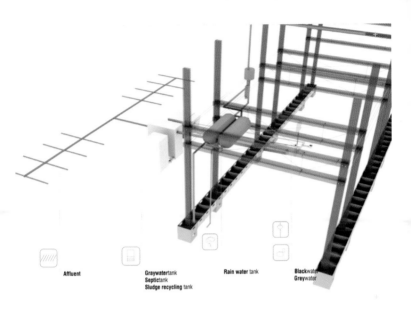

Affluent

Graywatertank
Septictank
Sludge recycling tank

Rain water tank

Blackwater
Greywater

ef002	City Seed	CH

Tosh Drake	Architect	tosh.drake@gmail.com
	NA_USA	University of Oregon

Modular dwelling provides food, water, and energy:
- Adaptive assembly system promotes evolutionary housing structures.
- Power provided by fuel cell supplemented by photovoltaic array.
- Rain water and grey water stored separately for drinking, bathing and irrigation.
- Hydroponics agriculture provides kitchen garden and market crops.
- City Seed systems are demountable, to be re-assembled in alternate configurations for migratory and evolutionary installation.

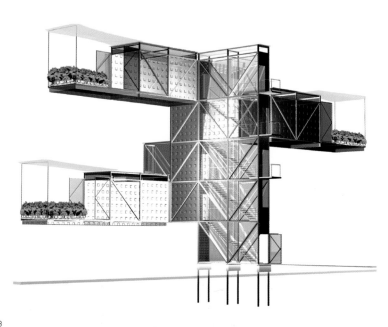

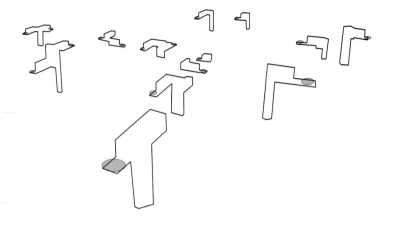

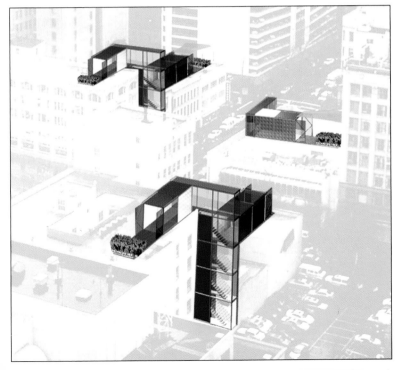

| 5.16 | 73f6d | Sustainable Fu-t(o)urism | CH |

| Emanuel Giannotti
Davide Fornari | Architect | etnografo@libero.it |
| | EU_Italy | IUAV, Venezia |

Sustainable Fu-t(o)urism is a self-sufficient collective housing project which aims to host tourists in the Venice area in a more sustainable way. Since tourism has become a phenomenon of the masses, it has a deep impact on the environment of tourist destinations: in several seasonal occasions the number of people in Venice becomes twice of its inhabitants and the city becomes a "caravanserai." We propose a new concept of luxury: tourism can be the occasion for "housing research." Our project is a resort where one can experience awareness. The main structure is a concrete, artificial ground on stilts. The wood dwellings are built with a timber-frame structure. The typologies of dwellings are minimally designed. We used four synthetic pieces of furniture designed by Bruno Munari.

Every dwelling has a patio and integrated technical solutions to provide the necessities for the whole building: a tank for collecting water, a photovoltaic system, solar collectors, and a solar chimney.

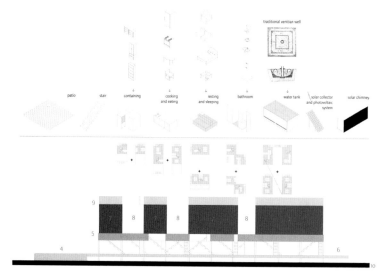

1 dock and reception 2 restaurant 3 laundry 4 artificial wetland 5 artificial ground 6 paths 7 dwellings 8 patios 9 solar chimneys 10 lagoon

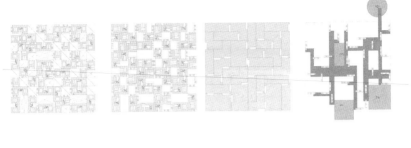

7d6S1 Plug-in House SH

– Francis Wilore	– Student	– fewltu@hotmail.com
– Todd Hochstetler		
	– NA_USA	– Lawrence Technological University

Our framework (SYSTEM) is a simple steel frame that can be configured to fit any site or environment. The basic frame is consistent, level upon level with an open, central core and containers plugged-in at the exterior. The SYSTEM can become part of the larger NETWORK of utilities or can add its own self-sustaining features as necessary. With the system in place, the residents are free to insert their homes (PLUG-IN). The PLUG-INS can be configured in multiple ways to adapt to the resident's needs, which might range from temporary disaster relief to long term family housing.

The containers would be outfitted with the necessary equipment to literally plug into their system's utilities and be ready for living. The shipping containers are modified to be combined. As a wall is removed on the exterior, it is re-used on the interior. Nothing is wasted. By removing the exterior and combining multiple containers, freely flowing open spaces are created.

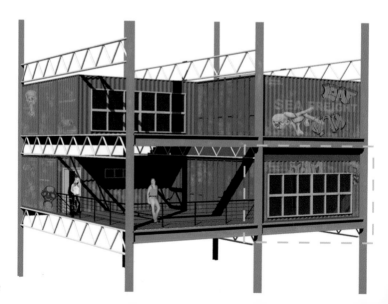

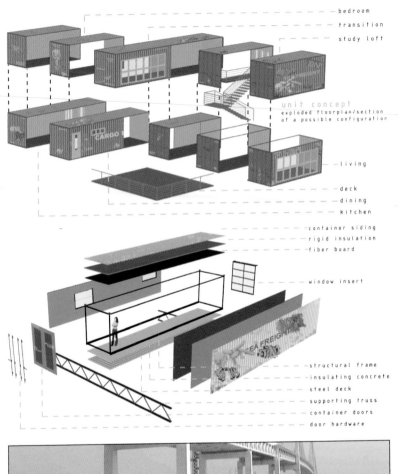

bedroom
transition
study loft

unit concept
exploded floorplan/section
of a possible configuration

living

deck
dining
kitchen

container siding
rigid insulation
fiber board

window insert

structural frame
insulating concrete
steel deck
supporting truss
container doors
door hardware

Guillermo
Garcia Badell

Student   guille_gbadell@yahoo.es

EU_Spain   ETSAM, Madrid

Nowadays 80% of the world's population lives in cities, resulting in the use of more than 70% of the energy produced worldwide. City and energy can't, therefore, be separated from each other.

The site of this project is a large field of olive trees that is arranged in a strong geometrical grid for production purposes. The intention is not only to respect this grid but also use it as a generator.

The housing development, with accompanying solar panels and other structures (explained thoroughly in the graphic documents), insert themselves into the olive tree grid. The housing units are conceived as independent modules that can be joined and combined to offer several solutions within the grid: a community living between olive trees, one that is still productive. As a grid this proposal may be extended infinitely, so housing can join with re-forestation strategies, blending two normally separated activities and making both more profitable.

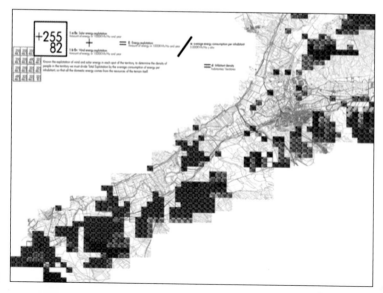

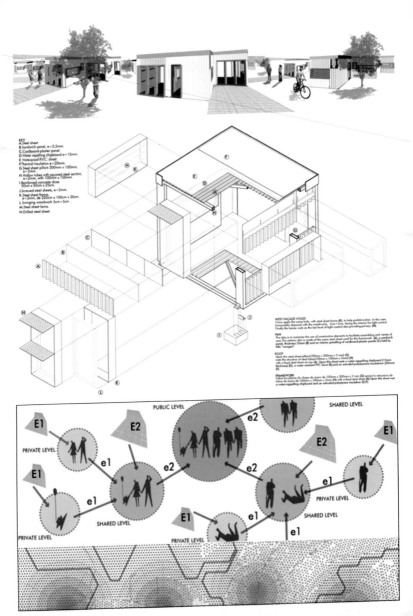

KEY
A. Steel sheet.
B. Sandwich panel, e=3,5mm.
C. Cardboard-plaster panel.
D. Water repelling chipboard e=15mm.
E. Waterproof PVC sheet.
F. Thermal insulation e=20mm.
G. Steel sheet pillars 300mm x 100mm, e=2mm.
H. Hollow tubes, with squared steel section, e=2mm, with 100mm x 100mm.
I. Reinforced concrete dices 50m x 50cm x 25cm.
J. Sawed steel sheets, e=2mm.
K. Steel sheet frame, e=2mm, de 2200mm x 100mm x 20cm.
L. Swinging woodwork 5cm x 5cm.
M. Steel sheet lama.
N. Drilled steel sheet.

WEST FAÇADE HOLES
Once again the same holes, with steel sheet frame (K), to help prefabrication. In this case horizontally disposed with the metalwork, 5cm + 5cm, facing the interior for light control. Finally, the lamas work as the last level of light control also providing privacy (M).

PLAN
The idea is to minimize the use of constructive elements to facilitate assembling and variety of uses. The exterior skin is made of the same steel sheet used for the framework (A), a sandwich panel, thickness 35mm (B) and an interior panelling of cardboard-plaster panels (C) held by tabs "setagas".

ROOF
Upon the steel sheet pillars (100mm x 300mm x 2 mm) (G) rests the structure of steel tubes(100mm x 100mm x 2mm) (H) with a fixed steel sheet on top (A). Upon this sheet rests a water-repelling chipboard (15mm thickness) (D), a water resistant PVC sheet (E) and an extruded polystyrene insulation (20mm) (F).

FRAMEWORK
Sobre los pilares de chapa de acero de 100mm x 300mm x 2 mm (G) apoya la estructura de tubos de acero de 100mm x 100mm x 2mm (H) with a fixed steel sheet (A) and an extruded polystyrene insulation (E,F).

PRIVATE LEVEL

SHARED LEVEL

PUBLIC LEVEL

SHARED LEVEL

E1   E2   e1   e2

2nd Prize Single Housing

Nicolas Buckley	Architect	chuba66@gmail.com
Kenny Orellana		
Carlos Arguedas	SA_Peru	Universidad Ricardo Palma

The city of Lima's poverty rate has increased from 31.9 to 34.7 percent. Independencia is a district that began as a populated settlement located in the outskirts of the city, to become located in the center of a great metropolis. Commitee 123 is part of a great set of housing structures located on the slopes of a hill, housing that was planned and constructed by its inhabitants. The proposal recognizes that for the adequate maintenance and production of the necessary resources (oxygen, water, energy, etc), interdependence between man, the environment and economic growth is indispensable. To elaborate an adequate interdependent method, the environment cannot become a tool for economic development. Instead, one should understand that if the environment is affected economic will cease. It is hard for companies or industries to accept this idea as valid. However, the poorer communities should be the sector being addressed.

For this reason, we believe that architecture should not be a completed object when presented to the inhabitant but rather it should be a product of various activities that allow progressive change, a cultural change that will be shown in future generations. It would not be wise to provide auto-sufficient objects to a population that has not yet considered the impacts of human activity on the environment.

We have elaborated 10 stages that will be developed in short and medium terms with the collaboration of the inhabitants of Committee 123 of the Independencia District:

First Stage: Municipal waste collection and recycling deposit
Second Stage: Pedestrian Access
Third Stage: Dry Toilets
Fourth Stage: Water nucleus
Sixth Stage: Oxygen production
Seventh Stage: Life nucleus
Eighth Stage: Alternative Crops and Urban Livestock
Ninth Stage: Basic Furniture
Tenth Stage: Information and entertainment nucleus

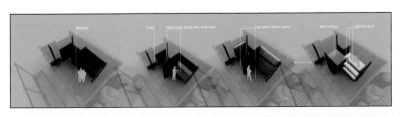

Natural rocks used for construction

Commitee 123

Actual pl

Country: PERU
City: Lima

District: INDEPENDENCIA
Community: 123

Altitude: 13.00 mt
Latitude: -12.0°
Max.Temp.[C°]: 29.0
Min.Temp.[C°]: 12.8
Rainfall [mm]: 0.0

Independencia
Lima Center

Recycling deposit

50 mt aprox

Actual stairs - Do not follow proper measures

SECTION

Actual dwelling module

Actual water reservoir

Commitee 123
36 FAMILIES
27 ACTIVE FAMILIES

uan Espinoza Falcon
ictor Allccahuamani Quispe
ixto Inca Poma
rlinda Allccahuamani Quispe
aulina Espiritu
ictor Salas
ario Guzman
urelia Arelano
miliano Lopez
lejandro Ponte
eltron Cueva
ederico Laberian
rancisco Zamudio
rlando Guevara
aure Ponte
estor Laberian
eor Gabrill
aruja Huaman
lejandra Huashuayo
orge Bizarraga
riseldo Dominguez
edil Izaguirre
eonidas Salas
suncion Reyes
eoncio Izaguirre
eguelina Goona
ery Huashuayo

FERTILIZER GENERATION   OXYGEN GENERATION
ALTERNATIVE CROPS   R RECYCLING
URBAN CATTLE RAISING

RECYCLING DEPOSIT

ELECTRICITY GENERATED FOR »
Information and entertainment nucleus

DWELLINGS NET PEDESTRIAN
[committee 123]

TRADE CENTER + Alternative
Crops and Urban Livestock

VEHICLE WAY

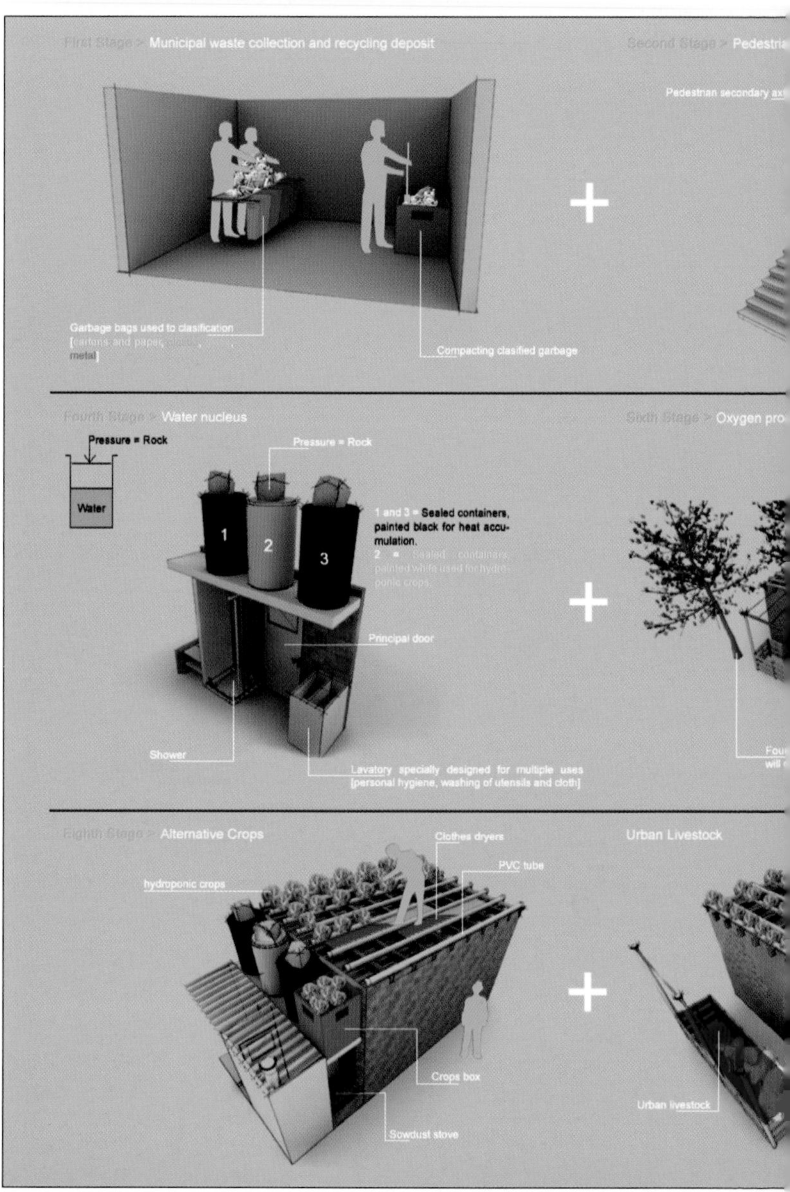

Pedestrian secondary axi

Garbage bags used to clasification
[cartons and paper, glass,
metal]

Compacting clasified garbage

Pressure = Rock

Water

Pressure = Rock

1 and 3 = Sealed containers,
painted black for heat accumulation.
2 = Sealed container,
painted white used for hydroponic crops.

Principal door

Shower

Lavatory specially designed for multiple uses
[personal hygiene, washing of utensils and cloth]

Fou
will

Urban Livestock

hydroponic crops

Clothes dryers

PVC tube

Crops box

Sowdust stove

Urban livestock

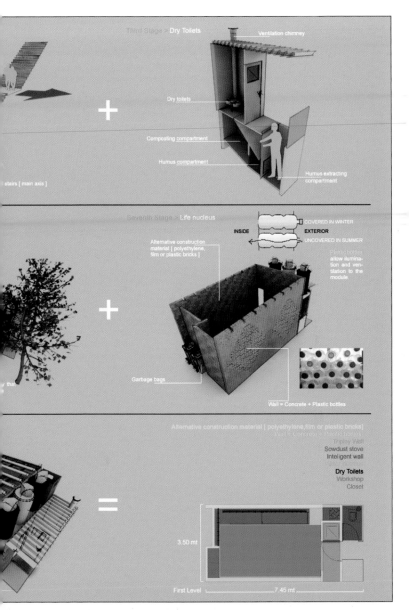

Ventilation chimney

Dry toilets

Composting compartment

Humus compartment

Humus extracting compartment

stairs [main axis]

+

COVERED IN WINTER

INSIDE

EXTERIOR

UNCOVERED IN SUMMER

Plastic bottles allow ilumination and ventilation to the module.

Alternative construction material [polyethylene, film or plastic bricks]

Garbage bags

Wall = Concrete + Plastic bottles

+

Alternative construction material [polyethylene, film or plastic bricks]
Walls : Concrete + Plastic bottles
Triplay Wall
Sowdust stove
Inteligent wall

Dry Toilets
Workshop
Closet

3.50 mt

=

First Level _____ 7.45 mt _____

74e33	S.E.E.D.		SH
Jorge Ramos	Architect	metalicwhite@rediffmail.com	
	CA_Cuba		

More than an approach to sustainable housing, S.E.E.D. is an approach to SUSTAINABLE LIVING. The model takes advantage of cutting edge technology to mimic some of Nature's most ancient knowledge. It takes a cue from the way photosynthetic organisms gather, process and store energy. It manages water using natural filtration systems. It collects and shares INFORMATION to ensure the most efficient performance and is capable of passing it on to the next generation.

S.E.E.D. units perform as a catalyst for ENVIRONMENTAL REMEDIATION AND ECOSYSTEM RECOVERY. The housing units have a FILTER EFFECT for human activities and their interaction with the environment.

S.E.E.D. units are modeled after LIVING ORGANISM (purple non-sulfur photo-synthetic bacteria). They are designed to populate with a POSITIVE OUTPUT in the ECOLOGY and SOCIAL system, providing BIOLOGICAL REMEDIATION, FOOD SOURCES AND ENERGY.

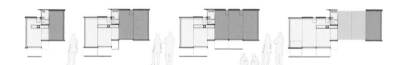

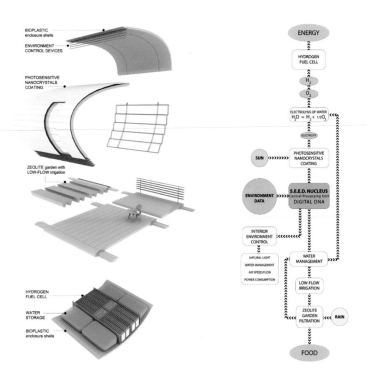

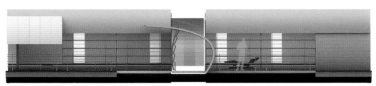

NORTH ELEVATION SCALE 1:100

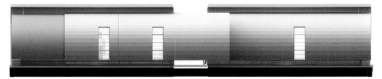

SOUTH ELEVATION SCALE 1:100

Position and Site

The house is not oblivious to its position, much less heedless of its surroundings; it is, rather, inseparable from its constitution together with the place.

The configuration of the self-sufficient dwelling is, more than any other, inherent to the site on which it is located, redefining it in some cases, entering into a harmony that favours the place or shakes it up, producing a positive impact by means of its inclusion.

It is then like the most domestic of exercises in that it is more closely related to the traditional stability of the house, to permanency, while declaring its capacity to add new conceptions to the environment which also produces it. Added but not foreign, Position and Site finds its self-sufficiency by means of close collaboration with the territory to which it belongs, a physical undertaking with the capacity to change and adapt to the landscape, to opportunity. As a result, it is equally effective, forceful and competent in urban and natural settings, and in every case it is governed by its adaptation to them.

Sometimes the dwelling may be found in unusual locations, like emergences from the ocean, an archipelago of anchored islands, L.o.W. Land, which extends its territory towards the water, colonizing a place that remains unchanged.

It may also be positioned according to structures; Urban tourism is a self-construction device mounted on urban communication infrastructures such as bridges.

Side grade adheres to a structure as though fitted to a residual end wall, temporarily sharing and working together with installations networks in the urban fabric.

It recycles and employs vertical interstitial spaces that were previously unused and underestimated by the city.

Rooftop Forest, conversely, can be sited on the terrace roof of any existing building, highlighting the qualities of its implantation.

Winner of third prize in the Self-Sufficient Single Housing Contest, it addresses the landscaped roof not as the conventional two-dimensional flat green space, but as a three-dimensional space with the power to redefine the skyline in which it is set.

It also uses the cycles of air movement in the urban fabric and harnesses the convection produced by the surrounding buildings as an element of temperature control and thermal efficiency, a greenhouse-cum-chimney, emulating the air currents in a forest as it produces the form.

| 2fc6a | Scrap House | | SH |

| Nutthawut Piriyaprakob | Architect | nuttha_p45@yahoo.com |
| | AS_Thailand | Ball State University, Indiana, USA |

SCRAP HOUSE Manipulating construction scraps for housing via digital technology. The scrap house is an experimental project that tries to prove how new digital technology can handle local materials, from around the world, for architecture. So, why not use a ton of scraps from gigantic construction sites to design, analyze, fabricate and construct by using current technology? Is such a thing possible?

Hopefully, I believe that this project will be a prototype for local architects to develop their own ideas to use any materials for architecture that is cheap, beautiful and practical.

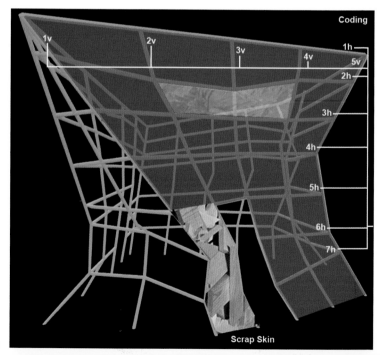

Coding

Scrap Skin

03a70 Housing at the museum

- Xavier Sanchez Valladares - Claudia Espinosa - Pyung-Yang Lee - Bea Etayo - Tasos Karamitsios	- Architect - NA_Mexico	- x.sanchez@lycos.co.uk - Bartlett School of Architecture / Universidad Iberoamericana, A.C.

Location: the Weald & Downland Open Air Museum, West Sussex, England.
Inspired by: Stonehenge. The houses are envisioned as irregular semi-buried stones emerging from the landscape. The internal environment will benefit from the super-insulated, thermally massive construction. This will result in more stable internal temperatures than in lightweight buildings.
The ambivalence between the north-facing slopes, towards the need for south-facing solar access, is synthesized into a "ying-yang" scheme. The south-facing wing has the bedroom areas looking onto a private underground 'greenhouse,' while the common areas are facing the exterior view of the valley. The dormitories use direct solar gains and pre-heated air rising from the underground courtyard. Hot air 'naturally' circulates all around the exposed thermal mass of this wing. The north living/dining/kitchen area is heated indirectly by the heat produced by a photovoltaic (PV) roof. The design not only responds to the site condition but also to the different occupational times of the dwelling. Each area has a specific strategy.

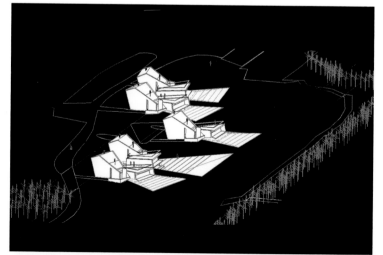

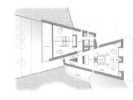

first floor

ground floor

section through the greenhouse

east elevation

west elevation

3e23e	Saving the forest	5H

├ David Vernet	├ Architect	├ vernet.d@gmail.com
	├ EU_France	

This proposal is not so much about self-sufficiency, but rather investigates interdependence and the acceptance of a common responsibility, through the resolution of a paradoxical situation: the ever growing number of recluse houses in Southern Europe, often a contributing factor to forest fires, might become a solution. These houses, scattered throughout the forest, participate in a shared duty: they form a network; they are units that function on several levels. They ensure the maintenance of neighboring forests; they offer fire-prevention watchtowers; they become water supplies and refuges when first aid is needed. In extreme situations, they offer a safe, fireproof haven for their inhabitants.

Each house is conceived according to low-tech ecological techniques such as material selection, waste recycling, renewable source of energy, passive insulation, optimized orientation, natural ventilation. The swimming pool is the central element, simultaneously dramatic and useful.

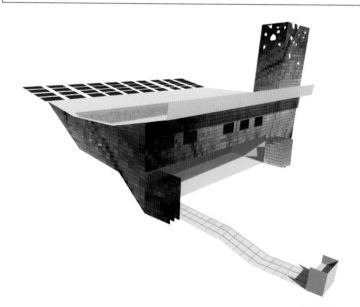

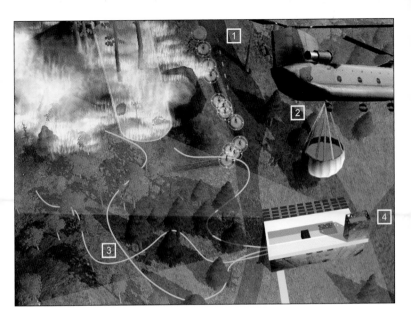

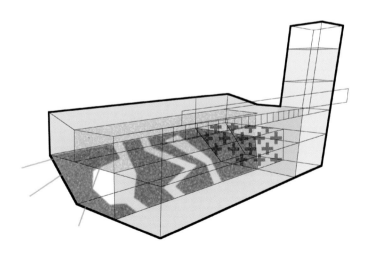

4d87e DIS/RE-assemble SH

| Juliet Hernandez Jhaelen Eli | Student | julen@generaldesignoffice.com |
| | NA_USA | Harvard Graduate School of Design |

In the United States, the new construction of a typical 1,700 sq.ft. wood frame house requires the wood equivalent to one acre of forest. Demolition is the main contributor to the material waste created by the AEC industry, with an estimated 150 to 250 tons of waste generated for the demolition of each average-sized residential dwelling.

While much emphasis has been placed on the reduction of material waste in new construction and the subsequent reduction in energy consumption during the life of a house, little attention has been paid to the "recycling" of existing houses slated for demolition.

DIS-assemble/Re-assemble investigates the opportunities inherent in the deconstruction and reconstruction of the single detached dwelling.

The manipulation of existing modules into new figures that respond specifically to energy consumption, water conservation, site specificity, economic imperatives, and programmatic requirements culminates in the creation of new relevant typologies and provides us with the opportunity to reinterpret conventional house forms.

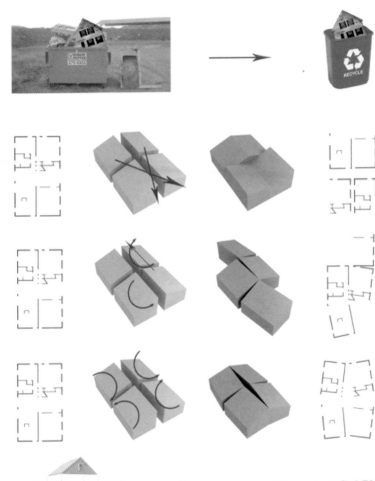

6ecb7

Hydroponic Bamboo Village

CH

Roderick Tong Lawrence Wong Bianca Cheung	Architect	roderick_tong@yahoo.co.uk
	EU_UK	Bartlett School of Architecture

We propose the creation of a self-sufficient community that consists of repetitive modules that operate their own water cycle by means of renewable energy and that is constructed from readily available, local materials, with minimum technological input.

The proposal consists of two interlinked systems. The Hydroponics Wastewater Purification System, located at the edge of the estuaries and partially submerged in the water, and the Hexagonal Bamboo Dwelling Units, which consists of Dwelling Units, water-related infrastructure and communal spaces.

Water is purified in two ways: 1– In the hydroponics wastewater purification system, contamination is removed by the roots of the aquatic plants. 2– In the water-related infrastructure, rainwater is harvested in the Hexagonal Cone, filtered, and finally stored in underground ferro-cement water storage tanks.

Each above-ground, elongated hexagonal cone protruding from the wooden planks, is a separate dwelling unit intended for as a private resting area. The wooden platform provides circulation and interaction spaces between families and individuals. The Hexagonal Bamboo Cones are communal spaces for activities related to water utilities.

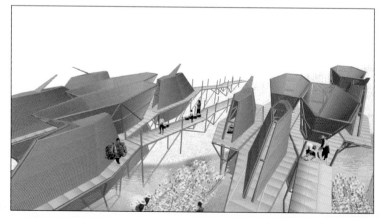

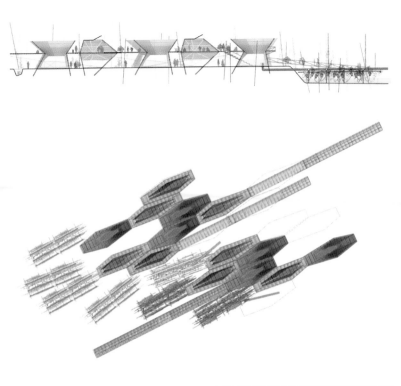

Rujun Xie
MAOAMO

Student
AS_China

xrj04@mails.tsinghua.edu.cn

Tsinghua Univesity

Human habitation design for scientists on Diaoyu Island.
Progress needs large quantities of research. It will solve the problems caused by the energy crisis.
The site is the island of Diaoyu in the East China Sea, the program was to design a building for research into oceanography, meteorology and physics, expeditions, and so on. The designed building can provide more than 40 rooms for scientists, every room is about 40 squares meters with simple furniture. During the day, windows will be uniformly open; at night, the windows will be closed because of the rising tide.
The glass is strong enough to withstand a fierce attack. The bath room is the heart of the room.

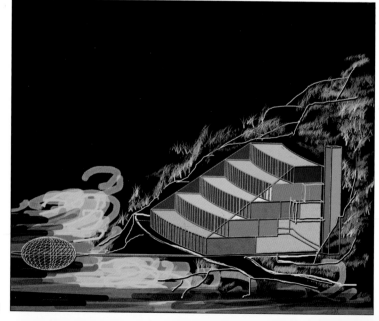

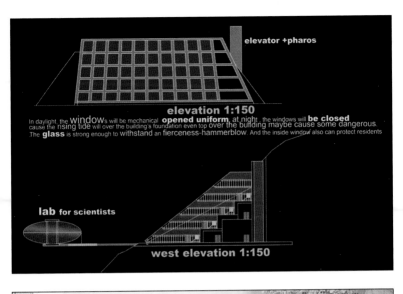

elevator +pharos

elevation 1:150

In daylight, the windows will be mechanical **opened uniform**, at night , the windows will **be closed** cause the rising tide will over the building's foundation even top over the building maybe cause some dangerous. The **glass** is strong enough to withstand an fierceness-hammerblow. And the inside window also can protect residents

lab for scientists

west elevation 1:150

| –Louise Jalilian –Petra Thedin –Koen Kragting | – Architect | – louise_jalilian@hotmail.com |
| | – EU_Sweden | |

Water is becoming a bigger threat to our conventional way of living. This project deals with living in flood areas and in waterzone with tide differences. We introduce a new attitude towards "living on the waterfront." The dwellings will be totally self-sufficient, their connection to the existing infrastructure making daily life more convenient. This connection is translated in the form of a pole. We introduce a new waterscape, formed by these energy producing poles.

The idea is to create 'pole-communities' in many waterfront areas worldwide. Rest energy created by the pole-communities can be used in traditional cities. The dwelling consists of three elements: a private, a social, and a service-unit, all connected to the pole. The sensitive relation to the water is negotiated on specific places in the dwelling. Folding walls and shifting floors generate a unique openness and a different experience of the water.

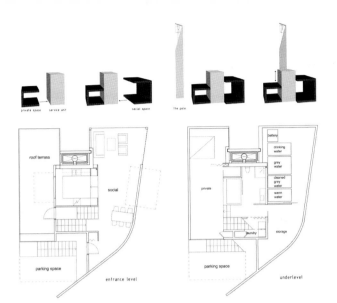

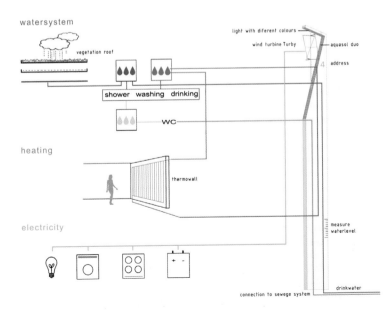

902f0   Place Station   SH

| Borrull Llobel | Architect | llobell2024@hotmail.com |
| | EU_Spain | ESCALArquitectes |

A house like a levitating parasite, taking all it needs from its environment...
The project is understood as a device, allowing:
-The setting in any kind of environment.
-The adaptation on the climate: thanks to the suppleness of its front.
-To capture needed climatic resources: sun, wind, and rain water by integrated capture systems.

STRUCTURE 1– The two parallel masts act in tandem to support to the structure's top, which houses equipment for wind capture and solar panels.
2– The platform serves as a support for the whole house. This strategy reduces the environment impact with the ground.

SUN BOX Captures required energy to heat water and to generate the necessary amount of electricity needed to power the structure's electric devices.

WATER LAYER Allows for the accumulation of rain water, enough an entire year.

WIND SPHERE Captures wind energy and transforms it into useable energy for the house.

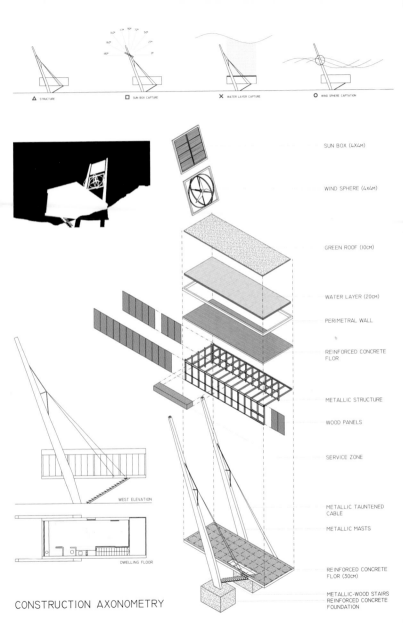

△ STRUCTURE   ☐ SUN BOX CAPTURE   ✕ WATER LAYER CAPTURE   ◯ WIND SPHERE CAPTATION

SUN BOX (4X4M)

WIND SPHERE (4X4M)

GREEN ROOF (10CM)

WATER LAYER (20CM)

PERIMETRAL WALL

REINFORCED CONCRETE FLOR

METALLIC STRUCTURE

WOOD PANELS

SERVICE ZONE

METALLIC TAUNTENED CABLE

METALLIC MASTS

REINFORCED CONCRETE FLOR (30CM)

METALLIC-WOOD STAIRS
REINFORCED CONCRETE FOUNDATION

WEST ELEVATION

DWELLING FLOOR

CONSTRUCTION AXONOMETRY

| 02396 | Housing in Lybia | | 5H |

| Muftah Abudajaja | Architect | mbudajaja@yahoo.com |
| | AF_Libya | Budja Design |

The house is divided into two parts or units: one for sleeping and one for living. The design is based upon the following points:
1– An inner courtyard for ventilation and light purposes. 2– The smart use of spaces according to the location. 3– Length and height measurements will vary to create roofs and shade. 4– The use of plants to renew, purify and perfume the air. 5– The use of water surfaces in the northern portion of the building to cool and refresh the air inside.
I consider that the most significant feature of the house is the simplicity and the clear use of spaces that are designated according to the night and daytime activity that mark the purpose of each room.

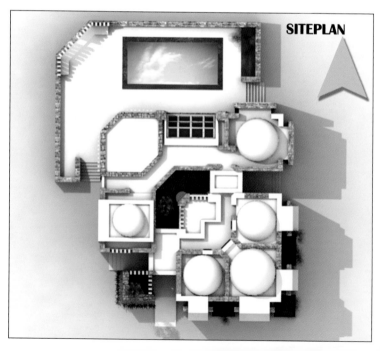

SITEPLAN

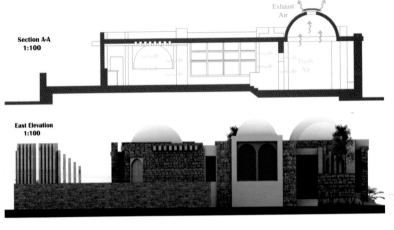

Section A-A
1:100

Exhaust Air

Fresh Air

East Elevation
1:100

West Elevation
1:100

5714e On a cliff side CH

| Anjit Chhatwal | Architect | a.chhatwal@gmail.com |
| | AS_India | University College London – The Bartlett |

I carefully picked a site along a cliff in Graz, Austria, where the temperature begins to drop in September and remains relatively cold until April. An habitat in such a locale would demand a large quantity of fuel to maintain a running life cycle. Using the concept of earth as a valuable incubator, I designed a housing system that is partially immersed in ground.

This immersion reduces the energy consumption of a typical household by 20%, because caves and other underground spaces are a few degrees above freezing point. I have designed a housing system where the available resources are recycled and used. Housed with single beds (Groups of two and three beds have been designed to form clusters). Each cluster is defined on two levels, connected by a paved area. These clusters are arranged in groups along the cliff, with the main connection space coming from within a carved earth cave, which is about 10- 15 m deep in places and covered with solar panels and glass.

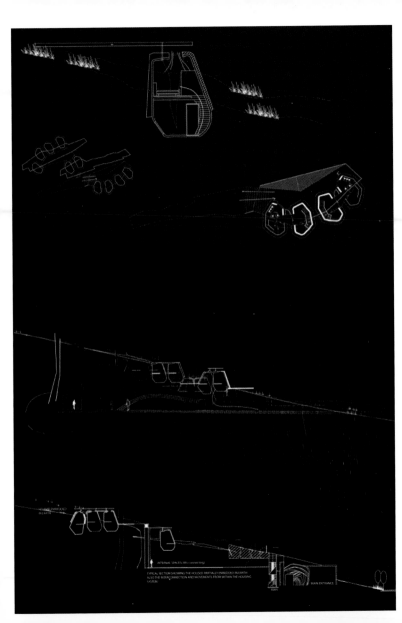

TYPICAL SECTION SHOWING THE HOUSES PARTIALLY EMBEDDED IN EARTH ALSO THE INTERCONNECTION AND MOVEMENTS FROM WITHIN THE HOUSING SYSTEM

MAIN ENTRANCE

27053 Cliff + Screen House

SH

James Pedersen
Russell Hodgkinson

– Architect — rjamesped@aol.com

– AC_Australia — University of Sydney

This submission proposes a sustainable and self-sufficient shelter located on the south-east Australian coast in an area traditionally owned by the Guringai people. It would accommodate two settlers who would normally have trouble surviving if unaided in such an environment. The shelter consists of a house and native working garden positioned on the ledge of an existing north facing cliff. It shares this ledge with an enormous spotted eucalyptus tree. At the base of the cliff directly below the tree is a natural water spring. The shelter is formed as much from synthetic materials as it is from utilizing parts of the surrounding natural environment.

The eucalyptus and spring below provide shade and water, the natural sandstone wall supplies the necessary bearing and thermal mass, while the full length adjustable screen that runs parallel to the cliff provides protection and thermal regulation to the occupants and native garden. Rainwater that falls on the site filters down to the spring.

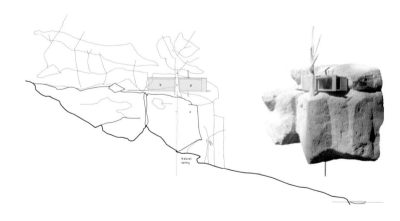

NORTH ELEVATION 1:200

a   Sandstone Cliff
b   Screen
c   Spotted Eucalyptus
g   Openable parts of screen
i   Waterline down to natural spring

CLIFF + SCREEN HOUSE
GURINGAI, AUSTRALIA   27053

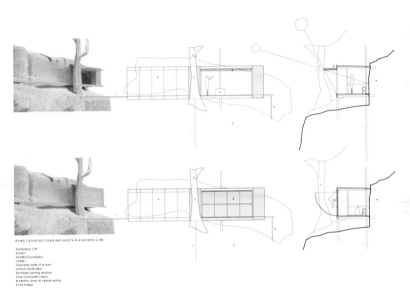

RXING CROSS SECTIONS AND NORTH ELEVATIONS 1:100

a Sandstone Cliff
b Screen
c Spotted Eucalyptus
d Ladder
e Openable parts of screen:
   vertical bifold steel
g full height awning window
h Slow combustion stove
i Waterline down to natural spring
j Entry bridge

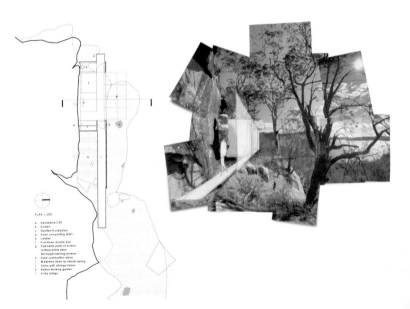

PLAN 1:100

a Sandstone Cliff
b Screen
c Spotted Eucalyptus
d Solar composting toilet
e Ladder
f Pull-down double bed
g Openable parts of screen:
   vertical bifold steel
h full height awning window
i Slow combustion stove
j Waterline down to natural spring
k Sinks with storage below
l Native working garden
m Entry bridge

Sarah Eldefrawy	Architect	sarah_eldefrawy80@yahoo.com
	AF_Egypt	Alexandria University, Egypt

The project goal is to create a healthy Mediterranean environment by using seawater as energy supply, mechanical pumping, and fresh drinking water. The design concept uses one main prefabricated unit, which contains all structural, electrical, mechanical, recycling elements.

1- Hydro-turbine electricity generating systems. The water can be piped from one level to a lower level. The resulting water pressure can be converted into mechanical and then to electrical energy. It also replaces the use of diesel fuel generators that have harmful effects in the environment.

2- Water wheel mechanical generating system.

3- Using solar energy to obtain fresh drinking water from salty water.

4- Water recycling room contains gravel and sand layers to partially filter grey water. Solids pass through a drying room to obtain organic materials for planting the garden.

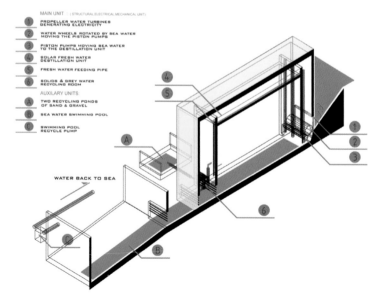

MAIN UNIT (STRUCTURAL ELECTRICAL MECHANICAL UNIT)

1. PROPELLER WATER TURBINES GENERATING ELECTRICITY
2. WATER WHEELS ROTATED BY SEA WATER MOVING THE PISTON PUMPS
3. PISTON PUMPS MOVING SEA WATER TO THE DESTILLATION UNIT
4. SOLAR FRESH WATER DESTILLATION UNIT
5. FRESH WATER FEEDING PIPE
6. SOLIDS & GREY WATER RECYCLING ROOM

AUXILARY UNITS:

A. TWO RECYCLING PONDS OF SAND & GRAVEL
B. SEA WATER SWIMMING POOL
C. SWIMMING POOL RECYCLE PUMP

WATER BACK TO SEA

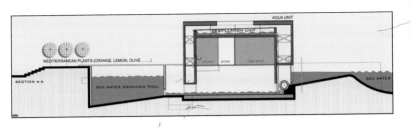

SECTION A-A

MEDITERRANEAN PLANTS (ORANGE, LEMON, OLIVE ......)

AQUA UNIT

DESTILLATION UNIT

SEA WATER SWIMMING POOL

SEA WATER

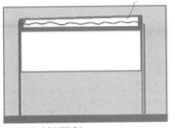

SOLAR CONTROL

MINMISING OF SOLAR HEAT
THROUGH ROOF BY USING IT
AS DESTILLATION UNIT

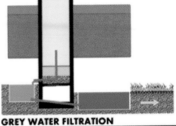

GREY WATER FILTRATION

3 STEPS OF GREY WATER FILTRATION
ONE IN THE MAIN STRUCTURE
AND THE OTHERS ARE TWO PONDS

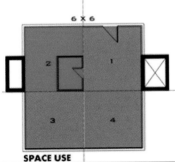

6 X 6

2   1

3   4

SPACE USE

ONE UNIT SPACE DIVIDED INTO
THREE SPACES USED ACCORDING
TO THE OWNER & KIT. +BATHR. UNIT

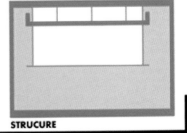

STRUCURE

FRAME SUPPORT ROOF & FLOOR
WITH TENSION CABLES

| – Simon Rastrorguev – Alexei Magai | – Architect | – x-4@narod.ru |
| | – EU_Russia | – YSTU |

The object is designed for the deserted and unpopulated districts of the Earth. The projected structure consists of a Shell covered with innovative absorbing combs. The Shell is necessary for protection of a cottage settlement against aggressive atmospheric phenomena. The Elementary cottages have a metal design and a covering of different types that carry out vital functions: processing solar energy to yield electrical, shielding heat-sink thermal (infra-red) energy, filtering water (with chlorophyll elements), and generating oxygen and water. Inside a Shell any atmospheric phenomena – rain, snow, wind and light effects – morning, day, evening, night can be created. These effects do not coincide with what occurs outside of a Shell, they are created at the request of the inhabitants. The Elementary cottage is designed for one family. The form of an Elementary cottage can be deformed in order to attach to different sites of a Shell.

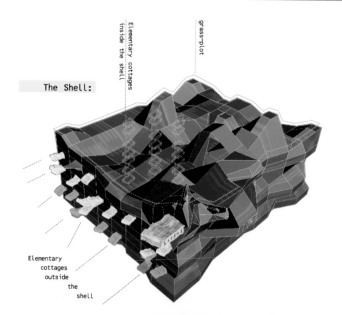

The Shell:

Elementary cottages inside the shell

grass-plot

Elementary cottages outside the shell

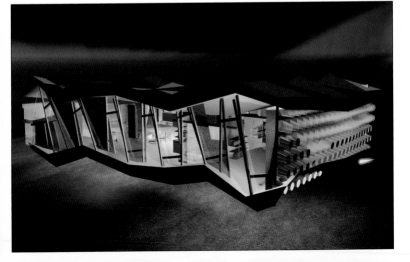

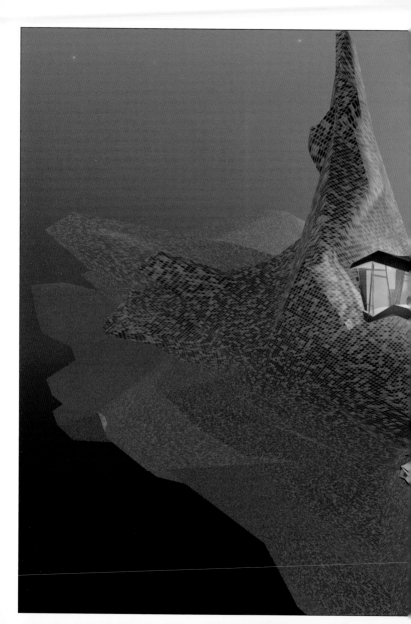

–Lucas Ruali –Mariella Tesse –Joao Neves Sobral –Carmen Zaghlou	– Architect – EU_Italy	– www.alsoavailable.net – info@alsoavailable.net – Also Available Architecture

"Additive" is an incubator for young creative people that share their strengths in order to avoid any kind of waste. It replies to the inadequacy of building typologies for people responding to the ID of the young creative class. "Additive" is conceived as a corroborator for old buildings and old behaviours. It re-activates human resources that would otherwise have higher social costs. It improves the quality of life of both buildings via a bilateral exchange of time and energies enabling ethic relations.

The idea is one of literally "attaching" a new building to an existing one to make it work better, empowering it with new sustainable technologies and new human energies, boosting the new building's technology in order to increase the old one performances.

| Rebeca Caso Donadei | Architect | rebecacaso@yahoo.com |
| | EU_Spain | |

The house wants to be with the organisms that inhabit this portion of the Mediterranean landscape. Where water can be scarce and summer heat uncomfortable, this house-organism combats climatic adversity by physically reacting to the environment. The building's metabolism makes sure that rainwater and the sun's rays are used in the most efficient way. In the winter, heat is obtained passively by opening up the shutters and large panels to the south, and actively by means of the solar panels situated on the roof, a second skin to the house-organism.

In the summer, heat is kept out by closing up the south facade while creating an outdoor living space in the shaded north side with those same elements that seal the structure in winter. At the center of the layout, the living space, visual and physical continuity between both worlds (summer and winter, interior and exterior) is attained.

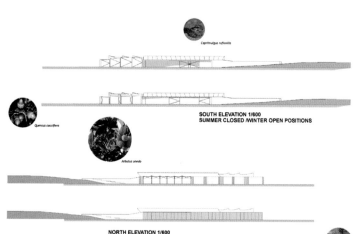

SOUTH ELEVATION 1/600
SUMMER CLOSED /WINTER OPEN POSITIONS

NORTH ELEVATION 1/600
SUMMER OPEN /WINTER CLOSED POSITIONS

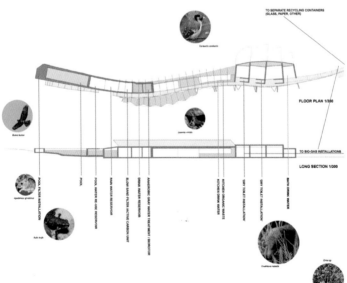

TO SEPARATE RECYCLING CONTAINERS
(GLASS, PAPER, OTHER)

Cerberris conberris

FLOOR PLAN 1/300

Buteo buteo

Lacerta viridis

TO BIO-GAS INSTALLATIONS

LONG SECTION 1/300

Apodemus sylvaticus

Bufo bufo

POOL FILTER INSTALLATION

POOL

POOL WATER RE-USE RESERVOIR

MAIN WATER RESERVOIR

SLOW SAND FILTER /ACTIVE CARBON UNIT

DRINK WATER RESERVOIR

ANAEROBIC GRAY WATER TREATMENT / BIOREACTOR

KITCHEN ORGANIC WASTE

KITCHEN DRINK WATER

DRY TOILET INSTALLATION

DRY TOILET INSTALLATION

BATH DRINK WATER

Oruithicus natalis

Erica sp

−Ricardo Guedes
−Francisco Ré
−Bruno André

− Student − sidegrade@gmail.com

− EU_Portugal − Universidade Lusiada do Porto

The project consists of a modular living structure occupying unused facades in the city, relating pre-existence with the new attachment. A prefabricated structure is attached to the blind facade. It is expandable allowing multi functionality and easy transportation. *Existenz-minimum* was privileged by a concentrated and mutating living space. The structure behaves as a system improving economic and ecological sustainability. Water is collected from the roofs; electricity is generated by solar panels placed on an articulated structure, one that also allows the placement of advertisement. The new structure provides an extra resource of water and electricity for the receptor building, as this one provides vertical property. Both buildings gain with the agreement, such as those buffaloes that allow birds to perch on their backs, while eating the bugs that infest their fur. The common expenses of a house are put aside thanks to a smart relationship of several systems and for the structure's exceptional site.

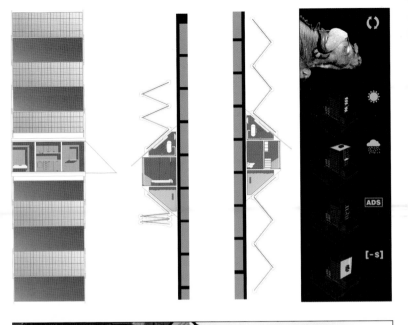

Fluid Space

–Tim Castillo Rana Abu-Daya	– Architect	– tbcastillo@hybridenvironments.com
	– NA_USA	– Columbia University

The fluid residence is a deviation from the conventional dwelling space. It attempts to understand self-sufficient housing within the realm of consumerism and information technology. It re-thinks dwelling through spatial dynamics and pushes technology to become more efficient. Sited in the landscape of the American southwest (New Mexico), the dwelling becomes an information center that transmits data electronically at several scales. Electronic consumer data is transmitted from the "fluid" billboard and loaded into GPS systems, cell phones and PDA's. This model allows the dweller to become "self-sufficient" by receiving his economic resources through paid advertisements displayed on the exterior skin of the residence.

Utilizing a mutant pin structure, the space can be redefined to conform to the ergonomic and performance criteria of the consumer. It derives its energy source from a photovoltaic panel system that functions both as a billboard and an energy collector. The systems within take on a self-sufficient condition by recycling gray water and minimizing expenditure of natural resources. In re-thinking how new digital and analog technologies influence cultural deviations, this speculative project embraces a more progressive exploration of habitation driven through hybrid information systems.

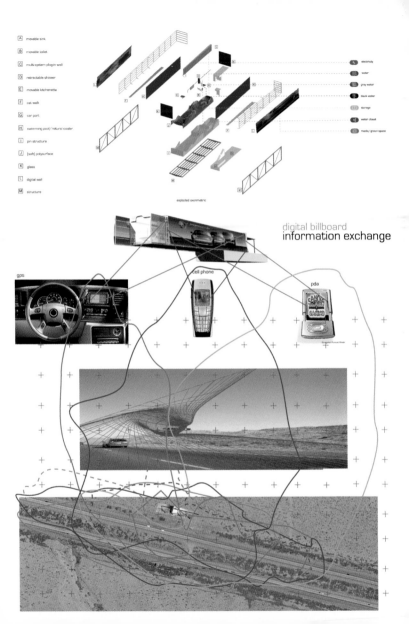

A movable sink

B movable toilet

C multi-system plug-in wall

D retractable shower

E movable kitchenette

F cat walk

G car port

H swimming pool/natural cooler

I pin structure

J [soft] polysurface

K glass

L digital wall

M structure

electricity

water

grey water

black water

storage

water cloud

media/green space

exploded axonometric

digital billboard
information exchange

gps

cell phone

pda

6.18	**d6bc5**	**Koolhouse**		**5H**

Dina Krunic	Architect	dinakrunic@yahoo.com
	EU_Serbia & Montenegro	UCLA, USA

Only 10% of the energy consumption in the built environment is used for electricity, 90% of our energy is spent on heating our houses! In order to maximize our energy resources we need to rethink how we heat our homes. Koolhouse is a proposal for rethinking a single family house layout based on the heat usage. This inspires a new classification of spaces of cold to cool, and warm to hot spaces. The bifurcation into two distinct layers, interior and exterior, develop gradients of heat agglomeration within their constituent zones. By exploding walls of the house into a thick space, we gain an inhabitable, in-between space, called "kool space." Kool space serves both as the daytime inhabitable cool space as well as air-based insulation for the warm spaces on the interior. This system integrates the greenhouse effect in the walls of the residential house, eliminates excessive insulation needs, and minimizes energy waste.

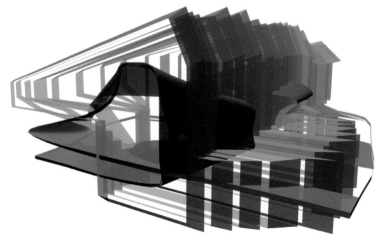

e82db   Rooftop Forest   5H

3rd Prize Single Housing

Yukio Minobe Etsushi Yamada Shinri Takano Chiaki Noto Shinichi Takahashi Hiroyoshi Matsumoto	Architect	yukio.minobe@gmail.com
	AS_Japan	

This eco-topography generates a comfortable environment only by the form and the arrangement of material.

1– Amplifying and Twisting the AIR STREAM

This architecture is designed as a device whose form amplifies the weakened wind by super high-rise buildings, TOKYO WALL. In summer, the interior is ventilated by chimneys assisted with the greenhouses (THERMAL CHIMNEY EFFECT) which in winter generate necessary heat (GREENHOUSE EFFECT). Furthermore deformation with the PRINCIPLE OF DRAFT strengthens air-flows to the interior and also to the leeward.

2– POROUS light structure and Foundation as a rainwater tank

Porous structure of wooden beams with CAD/CAM makes them lightweight and easily transported. The foundation of steel tubes serves as the rainwater tank.

3– Skin as an artificial landscape generating resources

The envelope is made of 6 kinds of GREEN pixels; a photovoltaic panel, a solar heat panel, and so on.

In this way, this project develops the new symbiosis device which uses contemporary urban environment slyly, at the same time improves the existing environment. Like a forest on the rooftop.

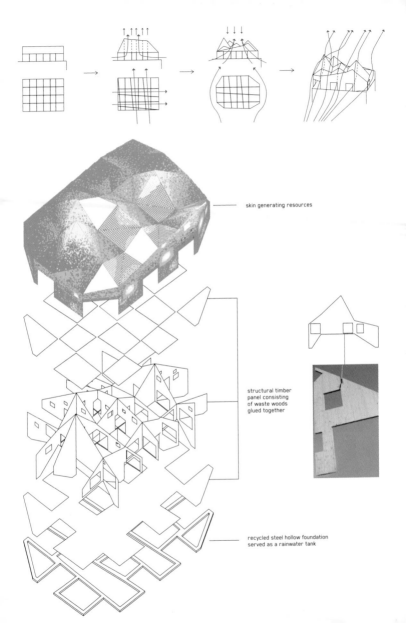

skin generating resources

structural timber panel consisting of waste woods glued together

recycled steel hollow foundation served as a rainwater tank

Summer D ay

In summer day, the thermal chimney warmed by the adjacent greenhouse draws out interior warm air towards the top and continuously absorbs cool air from outside. The air cooled by moss in the north side of a roof also is absorbed by the cool tube and furthermore cooled by the rainwater stored in the hollow foundation and send to interior. That rainwater under the floor also cools the room with a radiation through the plumbing of each floor and the roof with the showering. Electricity of those pumps is supplied by photovoltaic panels.

Summer Night

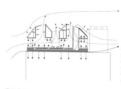

Hot Air ———
hello re Air r ———
cool Air ———

In summer night, the same system as day continues operating and night cool air is absorbed. The part warmed during noon miss heat forth and cools off.

Winter D ay

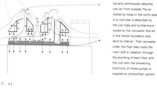

In winter, the greenhouses heat the interior air and accumulate heat in the walls and floors facing them. Furthermore, the greenhouses and solar panels heat the circulating rainwater in the floor and warms the room with radiation.

Winter Night

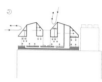

In winter night, the heat built in the walls and floors facing the greenhouses by day is released into the interior space, and blocks night cold air by this heat itself. At the same time, the hot water made by the greenhouses and solar panels warms the room with a radiation.

Rainy D ay

In rainy day, a chimney like a court collects rainwater as a funnel. Rainwater is stored in the foundation made by hollow steel tubes and is used for cooling the roof in summer, warming the floor in winter, and so on.

Sun ny D ay

In sunny day, photovoltaic panels generate electricity and solar panels heat stored rainwater and greenhouses generate hot air and grow plants.

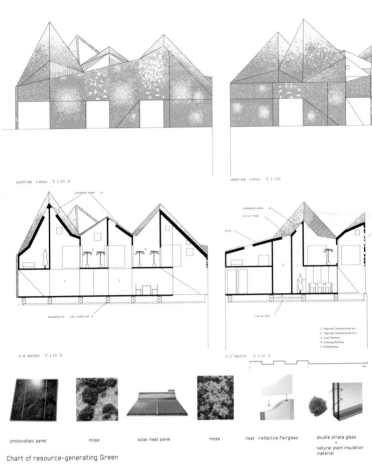

south ele vation S 1:15 0

west ele vation S 1:150

ventilation winds

ventilation winds
cool air inflow

moss

west l ray

foundation At rain water fan

cool air duct

a -a' section S 1:15 0

c -c' section S 1:15 0

1. Thermal Chimney/exterior l
2. Thermal Chimney/exterior l
3. Cool Chimney
4. Existing Rooftop
5. Greenhouse

photovoltaic panel

moss

solar heat panel

moss

heat -reflective Pairglass

double strata glass
+
natural plant insulation
material

Chart of resource-generating Green

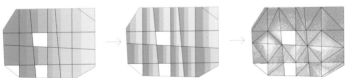

Growth process of Green according to the needed area and the direction and the movement
of the sun

Surfacial Diagram of the eco-topography

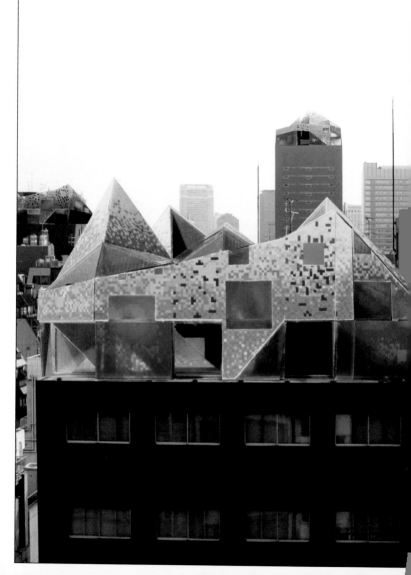

e8130 Flowing House

SH

- Filipa Valente
- Jorg Majer

- Student

- lipav@msn.com

- EU_Portugal

- Bartlett School of Architecture

Only 3% of the world's water is fresh water, with statistics indicating that it will eventually run out. The Flowing House aims to produce its own fresh water, drinkable and usable for essential needs. Considering that 97% of the world's water is saltwater the point was to take advantage of this unexplored resource. The house uses the technologies of desalination in a smaller scale and two different methods to obtain fresh water from seawater. The building is located in a coastal region and strategically positioned in a sloping terrain, ending in the sea, in order to use gravity for the processes. Seawater is pumped into a main reservoir by the user, and then redirected through a reverse osmosis channel where it is chemically filtered in order to be drinkable. Moreover, the remaining water is treated in distillation capsules and used for gardening or cleaning. The salt resulting from distillation is used as a construction material to extend the house outside.

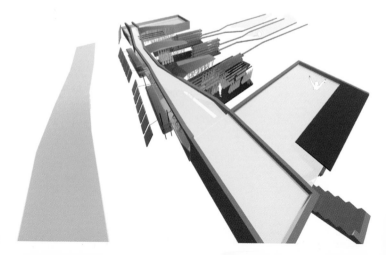

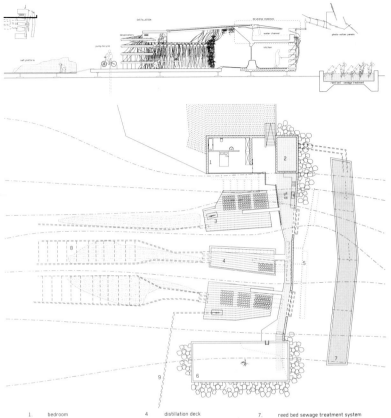

1. bedroom
2. reverse osmosis channel
3. bicycle water pump
4. distillation deck
5. photo-voltaic panels
6. swimming pool
7. reed bed sewage treatment system
8. salt platforms
9. sea water route in

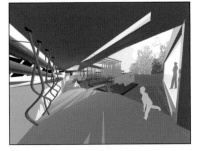

fc841 — Using natural sources — SH

| - Adriano Marchisciana
- Agostino Scuderi
- Giuseppe Montante | - Architect | - arch.msa@tiscali.it |
| | - EU_ITALY | - Università degli studi di Palermo |

Good, self-sufficient housing should be able to utilize energy sources. Our proposal wants to take into consideration the physiological behaviour of a plant, which lives through continuous physical reactions with the natural environment. Natural sources utilized: Natural thermoregulation. The house is encircled by deciduous trees that allow the passage of sunbeams during the winter.

These same trees create an efficacious natural screening during the summer. The cover of our housing consists of heat resistant panels. Under the floor of the housing, is a subterranean main that facilitates the entrance of the land breeze inside the housing. The land breeze is piped in through six conic air inlets which are directed towards the stream of the prevailing winds. The production of electric energy. The production of electric energy is guaranteed by some photovoltaic panels. The storage and reutilization of the rainwater. Waste water purification for irrigative reutilization through the use of swamp plants.

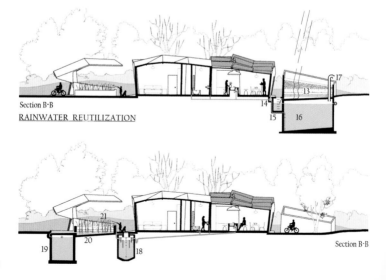

Section B-B
RAINWATER REUTILIZATION

Section B-B

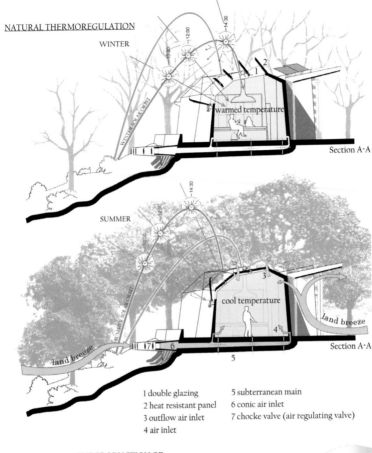

NATURAL THERMOREGULATION

WINTER

warmed temperature

Section A-A

SUMMER

cool temperature

land breeze

land breeze

Section A-A

1 double glazing
2 heat resistant panel
3 outflow air inlet
4 air inlet

5 subterranean main
6 conic air inlet
7 chocke valve (air regulating valve)

THE PRODUCTION OF ELECTRIC ENERGY

8 photovoltaic panels
9 electric net
10 overcurrent protection
   safety disconnected
11 battery
12 DC/AC inverter

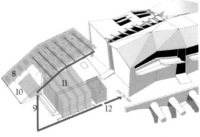

Models of self sufficient housing

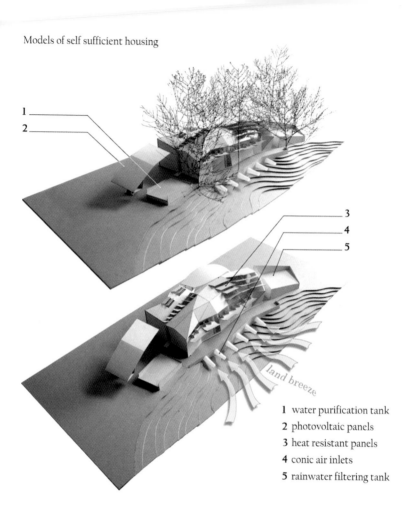

1 water purification tank
2 photovoltaic panels
3 heat resistant panels
4 conic air inlets
5 rainwater filtering tank

land breeze

North elevation

| – Elodie Nourrigat
– Jacques Brion
– Gaetan Morales | – Student | – efecampoy@hotmail.com |
| | – SA_Bolivia | – Universidad Católica Boliviana |

This project proposes a housing solution in the Bolivian Altiplano, where collective housing is also productive housing based on low income agriculture. A low cost system is proposed, so that heat can be used inside the housing through materials that absorb and distribute the heat.

Also we propose the use of bio-digesters which generate electricity, bio-gas for the housing and bio-fertilizer for the orchard. Self-sufficient collective housing, which uses alternative eco-environmental energies.

With a continuous wall of mud, we propose three dwellings for 6, 4 and 2 persons. The services modules are plugged into the housing block via a free plan and spatial distribution is configured by the user's appropriation with the flexible walls of cardboard tubes.

Finally, communal spaces are generated with the creation of a housing complex, where the objective is to remove the negative stigma of the mud walls, typically considered poor materials.

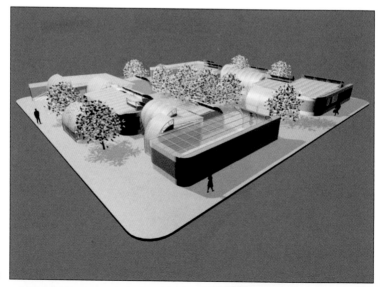

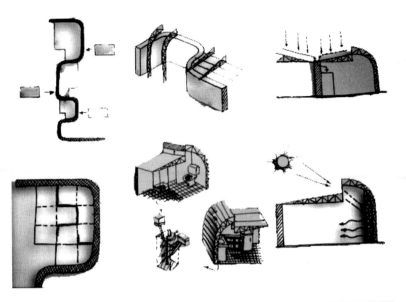

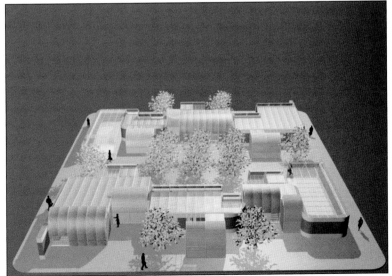

s9b6a **Self-Sufficient Shelter** CH

| Joana Rodrigues | Architect | joanatri@gmail.com |
| | EU_Portugal | Universidade do Minho |

The house considered as a simple shelter, using simple techniques in symbioses with the surrounding environment, receives the basic elements, uses them and then returns them back, cleansed, to nature. The roof leads the water through a downward pipe to a depository where it is treated and conducted for domestic use. This water depository is the main support structure of the house, giving it stability. Membranes in opposite sides of the house (back and front) direct wind energy into the micro-eolic turbines that produces electric energy for the household. The eolic channel reinforces the horizontal structure that constitute the rotation axisl of the unit modules, as well as distributing the house functions. The photovoltaic cells that coat the lateral faces allow visibility from interior to exterior, to usufruct the house's privileged position.

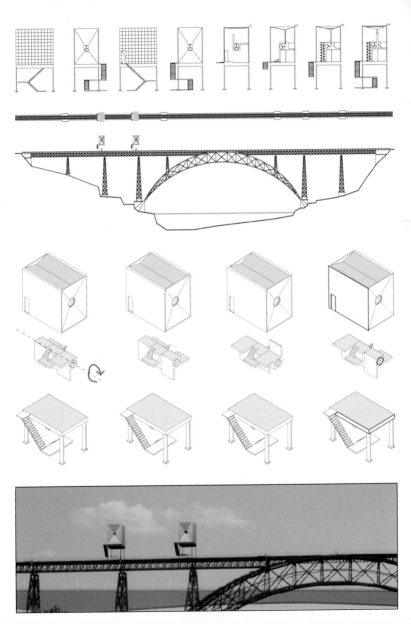

c76be   Sustainable Rooftops   SH

- Adam Mann
- Andrew Boger
- Amar Patel

- Student

- am000067416@ltu.edu

- NA_USA

- Lawrence Technological University

We decided to use a site that is present all over the world: building rooftops.
Natural ventilation and day lightning were major factors in the design of the
building. The overall form of the building is long and slender, wrapped around
the edge of rooftops. The slenderness of the buildings allows easy ventilation,
as well as day lighting in almost every room. The full glass windows would be
lined with moving louvers that would deflect lightning entering the building or
collect solar energy via photovoltaic cells, which would produce electricity
for the building. The concrete allows a concrete core conditioning system.
The heat gained through solar energy is distributed throughout the building
with the water floor system to ensure an even room temperature. The water
used in the concrete core conditioning system has been collected from the
rooftops. A water purification system would be installed in the building, so
that the sme water is used several times before it is expelled as waste. The
courtyard would consist of a large green space releasing oxygen and collecting water run-off.

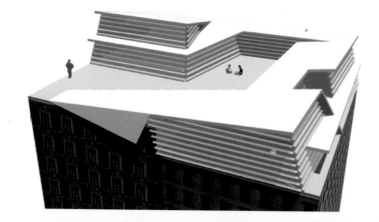

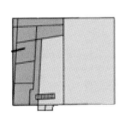 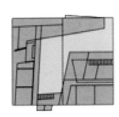 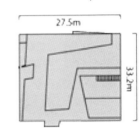

27.5m

33.2m

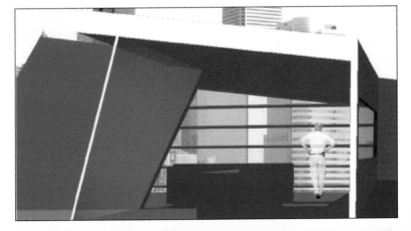

bSS31   Net-Cell   SH

| Rabindra Adhikari | Student | rabi.adhikari@gmail.com |
| | AS_Nepal | Nepal Engineering College, Bhaktapur |

What would happen if all the birds were to live in a single tree in the evening? Kathmandu shows an excellent example of integrated living environment. Housing being densely arranged in the core is surrounded by arable land. The housing units combine the living and commerce as a cell.

Information technology has redefined the work and house relationship. Within from the comfort of our living room, we handle business.

When work comes into the living room, distance seems meaningless. Integrated living environment makes people more independent of place and the meaning of proximity is defined with the bits and bytes of the information technology. Thus, "sustainability does not require a loss in the quality of life, but does require a change in mind – set, a change in values toward less consumptive lifestyles.

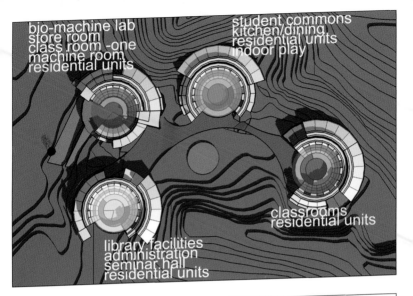

bio-machine lab
store room
class room -one
machine room
residential units

student commons
kitchen/dining
residential units
indoor play

classrooms
residential units

library facilities
administration
seminar hall
residential units

Territorial and Comunity

This category regards the house as part of a territorial set-up.

The dwelling freely decides to share a common space, as a result of which the preserve of the private domain goes on show. Establishing the community as an alternative, higher system of social organization is, then, inherent in this way of regarding the act of dwelling.

It is a way of determining, constructing and conceiving of intensely open and much frequented private space, at the same time shunning exclusion or marginalization.

The resulting space is one of addition to and integration with the dwelling where the occupier, and his or her habitation, develop as a member of a group, on a more social plane that is at times determined by relations of production and is wholly defining. In this way, social commitment, seen as a free form of elective relationship, is based on shared systems of tapping into resources, general programmes of sustainability and integrated management networks by means of a non-aggressive positioning and installation in the territory. This is a benefit that extends to all members of the community in collaboration with the environment.

By way of installation and reintroduction into the landscape, with an evaluation of its temporary nature, Landfill settler has recourse to the various gas bulbs produced by micro-organisms in lower strata of the site as an energy source for the home, with various lines of supply to the community.

It is actively involved in the inherent cycles of the place and proposes congruency and complicity between the parts.

Likewise, the Moisture patch basic unit is an

attendant approach that can be generalized and multiplied as a structure that purifies the water at the different levels of humidity in the subsoil and regenerates previously more arid land in territories with plant cover.

It is, then, a sustainable system of revitalization of the territory by means of the impact of the community, which turns the dwelling and its inhabitants into a mechanism of support, contribution and territorial service.

Industrial [+] garden [+] house presents the insertion of the greenhouse-housing complex into a run-down industrial fabric, while creating a new, regenerative landscape in interstitial spaces of the fabric and producing systems to process industrial air and waste by means of convection currents in the dwellings. The interstitial space becomes heterogeneous and accumulative as it is drawn into the fabric.

01d27 Landfill settlers

Eva M. Silberschneider

Architect

eva.silber@gmx.net

EU_Austria

University of Technology Graz

The project is grounded on the idea of reusing contamined areas. The problematic nature of these areas is a global issue and so is the selected site of the old Georgswerder landfill in Hamburg, Germany, which is just one of thousands. The contribution shows a possible scenario of settling the rehabilitated landfillarea, which evolved as a self-sufficient, settled community by docking the found technical installations on the site. For example, the existing gas extraction system maintains the energy supply. The water supply for the settler community is based on drainage in the landfill cover system. This concept is intended to be a temporary dwelling. Two different kinds of housing schemes will form a perfect symbiosis while extracting the noxious gases from landfill body. When the energy source is exhausted, the settler can move to the next one. The left area, covered with infrastructure, still holds great potential for future scenarios with a manifold of uses.

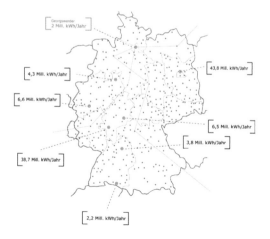

Georgswerder
2 Mill. kWh/Jahr

4,3 Mill. kWh/Jahr

43,8 Mill. kWh/Jahr

6,6 Mill. kWh/Jahr

6,5 Mill. kWh/Jahr

3,8 Mill. kWh/Jahr

38,7 Mill. kWh/Jahr

2,2 Mill. kWh/Jahr

⊚ examples of existing landfills with gas extraction system

• number of existing landfills in Germany
(356 in the year 2000, positions fictitious)

——— "landfill-hopping"

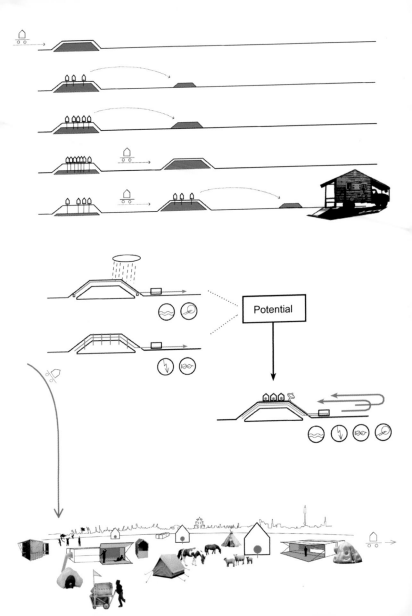

Potential

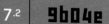 Trizone SH

−Kent Pedersen	− Architect	− kp@kent-pedersen.dk
−Mathilde Petri		
−Marie Preisler Berthelin	− EU_Denmark	− Kunstakademiets Arkitektskole, Copenhagen

Maximise the passive use of solar energy 1− Allow low winter sun into the rooms - avoid high summer sun. 2− Solar walls. 3− Thermal solar collectors. 4− Photovoltaic collectors.

Minimizing heat loss through the building skin 1− Compact building form with minimized vertical heat loss. 2− Exploit the principles of natural ventilation by the chimney effect as thermal regulator. 3− High level of thermal insulation; 300 in walls, 400 mm in roof and slab.

Optimizing the use of daylight (to minimize the use of artificial light)
1− East-west orientated rooms allow the low sun to enter far into the rooms.
2− Use of surfaces to reflect and direct light.

Use of recycled material and biodegradable and reusable building materials
1− Concrete, bricks and tiles.

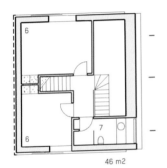

46 m2

- Hideyuki Natsume
- Sosuke Ito

- Architect

- natsume.hide@jp.fujitsu.com

- AS_Japan

- Kyoto University

This house consists of a series of exchangeable filter structures. The filters function not make up all elements of the house, but they also function as filters to purify various types of liquid, rainwater and human waste. Inhabitants of this house can make use of purified water for drinking or watering plants and crops.

Furthermore, the filter could function like a radiator and also be a key structure for thermal insulation.

The assembly of this house could function as moisture conditioning patches on the ground, like a cosmetic treatment masque.

Their use could transform drastic environments, like a dry land destroyed by human use, into a moist and comfortable territory for plants to grow and also for human beings.

As a result, the earth is revitalized by house units-patches.

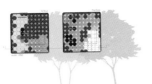

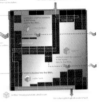

— Lukas Narutis | — Student | — aciulabai@gmail.com

— EU_Lithuania | — Vilnius Gediminas technical university

A man or a camel, staring at the stars above the desert, acknowledges how lucky they are to be there. A place to breathe and dream, absolutely free! Just one simple question bothers both of them: Do oases still exist, here on our lonely planet? The paradigm: "We should stand for a better chance for survival if we accommodated ourselves to this planet and viewed it appreciatively instead of dictatorially." Our idea of self-sufficient housing is based upon a principle that sustainable and economically profitable housing can be achieved with passive exploitation of natural environmental and climate resources, combined advanced IT and Hi-tech. The Oasis design idea is dictated by an aim to incorporate self sufficient maintenance systems: active (photovoltaic panels, solar collectors, heat pump, "living machine") and passive (energy saving, shading, conditioning, water collecting) into the minimal space of living buildings, without forgetting comfort and classical architectural aesthetics.

(Sun light path, shading, heat absorbtion)

Sun position durring SUMMER high

Sun position durring WINTER low

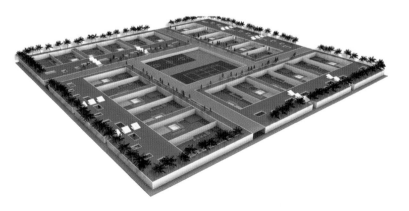

| –Olindo Merone
–Edoardo Boi
–Emanuele Pibiri | – Architect | – o.meronearchitetto@tiscali.it |
| | – EU_Italy | |

This investigation links the need for environmental comfort and a knowl-
edgeable "recovery" of building material through the use of a typological
system and a constructive process. The project is structured as a process
of composition and decomposition of a single housing complex: a device
able to integrate with recycled material, available on-site, and to involve
the inhabitants in a rediscovery and reinterpretation of their own ties with
the environment. The project intends to reduce the use of energy and raw
material consumed in the building process and wishes to guarantee excellent
environmental comfort by taking advantage of natural resources operating on the shape of the house and on the building process. The combination
of the several passive control systems and the adopted typological models
allows us to accomplish a process in which the protection of the biological
cycle becomes the way for form and content, typology and building process
coexisting as one.

continental climate_austria

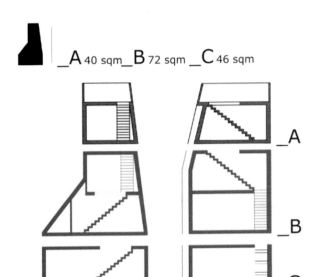

_A 40 sqm _B 72 sqm _C 46 sqm

longitudinal section   cross section

_A

_B

_C

desert_ niger

| Rychiee Espinosa Yu Brian Leung Scott Laporte | Architect | rychiee@hotmail.com |
| | NA_USA | Lawrence Technological University |

The current state of our culture results in our dependency on a single automobile. The availability of mass transportation has steadily decreased due to the spread of urban communities. As a result, non-renewable energy resources are being depleted, which could in turn cause a worldwide shortage of fossil fuels. Other energy sources need to be developed in order to circumvent the loss of fossil fuels and prevent further degradation of our ecosystem. In order to address this concern, we have developed a system which attempts to hold the single automobile captive, modifying the conventional residential parking space into something more ornamental. The automobile, led into each unit through a series of narrow ramps, is contained and integrated into the daily living space. In this case the automobile becomes sculptural in intent, rather than a traditional mode of transportation. As a consequence of the difficulties that arise when using the automobile, the user is encouraged to use mass transit and other means of transportation which ultimately results in the conservation of energy and valuable fossil fuels. As the structure's skin wraps around the building and meets grade, it folds to create a pedestrian transportation shelter which accommodates bicycle storage and provides access to local mass transportation.

photovoltaic

steel structural

glass curtain

existing

Controls are located inside the tenant space which allows the user to adjust the window and photovoltaic position in order to obtain the optimum solar angle of incidence.

The structure folds to create a pedestrian transportation shelter, which contains bicycle storage and access to local mass transportation.

Photovoltaic exterior skin is operable to capture maximum exposure to the sun, lowering energy consumption. Variations in the structural folds serve as additional fixed solar collectors.

The connecting structures provide supporting features such as market place, café, recreational activities, and other retail spaces.

In any given situation, the existing structure can be reused, lowering construction cost and waste, in both manufacturing and construction.

The roof system minimizes reflectance, which also acts as a filter for rain water collection to be used for utilities.

linkage

modular insert

[43% of our fuel is used while we're sitting still]

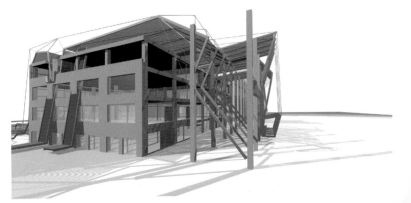

- Asaduzzaman Rassel
- Student
- asadrassel2004@yahoo.com

- AS_Bangladesh
- Bangladesh Uni of Engeneering and Technology

In this region, the pond plays a vital role in daily life. Almost every house has its own pond that is used for drinking water, washing and fishing. At the start of the rainy season, a portion of lands washed away with floodwater and so were the ponds. Residents lost their crops, cattle and poultry, nearly everything. Maybe these disasters can be avoided with some thoughtful, innovative, and cooperative design solution. **FIRST PHASE** The compound should be multi-clustered, built sharing one single area. Consisting of forty dwellings and an adequate stock pit sanitation system. **SECOND PHASE** The compound is raised from sea level to the maximum flood level of the area. **THIRD PHASE** The soil for the raised area comes from a big pond surrounded by the raised area sharing the water for the compound. **FOURTH PHASE** The compound guards against the wind with a green barrier that reduces the air pressure of the cyclone. **ENERGY EFFICIENCY** 1– Bio-gas. 2– Rainwater. 3– Solar panel. 4– Wind tower.

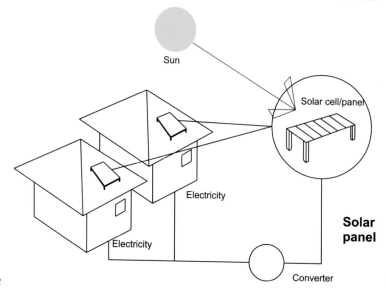

Sun

Solar cell/panel

Electricity

Electricity

Solar panel

Converter

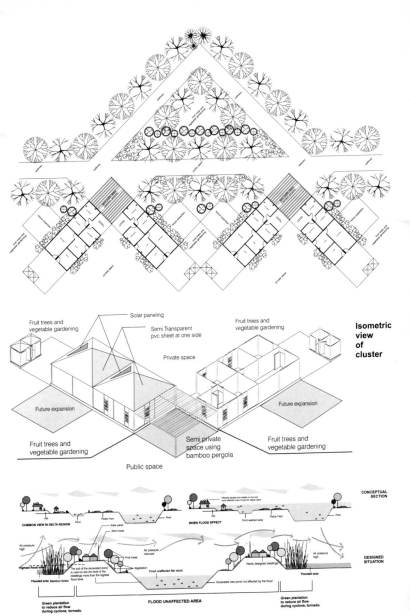

Isometric view of cluster

Fruit trees and vegetable gardening

Solar paneling

Semi Transparent pvc sheet at one side

Fruit trees and vegetable gardening

Private space

Future expansion

Future expansion

Fruit trees and vegetable gardening

Semi private space using bamboo pergola

Fruit trees and vegetable gardening

Public space

CONCEPTUAL SECTION

Pond

River

COMMON VIEW IN DELTA REGION

Elected people took shelter on the roof more effected area moved to higher place

Villa

Pond washed away

Paddy Field

River

WHEN FLOOD EFFECT

DESIGNED SITUATION

Air pressure high

Solar panel

Wind tower

Air pressure reduced

Fruit trees

The soil of the excavated pond is used to rise the level of the dwellings more then the highest flood level.

Vegetation

Flood unaffected fish stock

Newly designed dwellings

Excavated new pond not affected by the flood

Air pressure high

Highest flood level

Flooded area   Bamboo forest

Flooded area

FLOOD UNAFFECTED AREA

Green plantation to reduce air flow during cyclone, tornado.

Green plantation to reduce air flow during cyclone, tornado.

a1204 Sand & Salt

CH

Rop van Loenhout Ludo Boeije Dennis Moet Rickerd van der Plas	Architect	info@attika.nl
	EU_Netherlands	

The development of self-sufficient enclaves with symbiotic relationships between culture and nature: a cloud-like instead of clock-like approach. **SAND** reverses the encroaching formation of deserts through a 'nomadic recover machine'. On desert's edges a dune is formed using waste materials. The leeside provides an autarkic oasis made of recycled and light-tech materials attuned to local conditions. Strips of desert are covered with foil to reduce evaporation and conserve water which will then be used for re-vegetation and to produce energy. The oasis and her veil move on into the desert to repeat the process. **SALT** concentrates on rising sea levels and over-fishing of the world's seas with 'hybrid offshore living machines'. They consist of flexible living-working units around a central column in which the machinery is integrated. It moves with the tide and the rising sea level. Collection of rain and desalination of sea water produce drinking water.

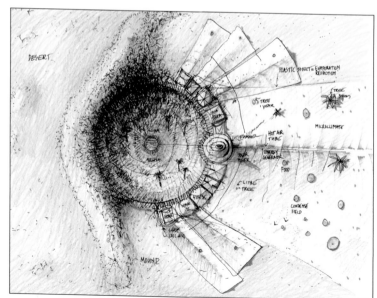

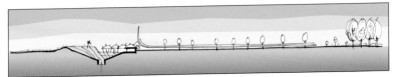

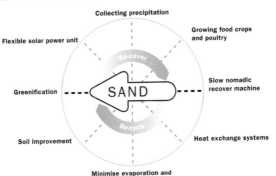

Collecting precipitation

Flexible solar power unit

Greenification

Soil improvement

Minimise evaporation and
usage of ground water

Growing food crops
and poultry

Slow nomadic
recover machine

Heat exchange systems

Re-cover

SAND

Re-cycle

LOW + ECO-TECH

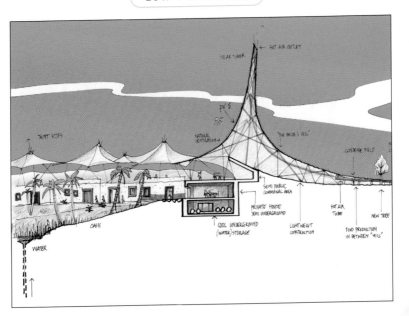

abSSf

Flowing through Boavista

CH

- Helio Boto
- André Miguel Lopes

- Student

- andremimoso@gmail.com

- EU_Portugal

- University Lusíada of Porto

Territorial cleansing, renewal and revitalization through an urban tissue integrated structure. The river has a strong bond to the city in its development across history, and like a winding, jungle river that generates life, feeds ecosystems, and creates habitats, so does our proposal winds through pre-existences. A combination between hi-tec (photovoltaic façade, biomass processing unit) and low-tec (crossed and vertical ventilation, greenhouses, plant façade) is fundamental in reducing the energy consumption, which combined with a modular constructive system that uses synthetic materials and pre-fabricated modules, reduces the over all impact of the whole building. The building works like a community promoting social responsibility through the shared greenhouses that are the responsibility of the inhabitants, also promoting dwelling spaces across the building. Within this spirit and integrating the new family unit concepts and different space appropriations, our building offers a wide variety of typologies as well as great spatial flexibility and mutability.

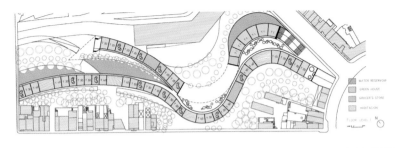

WATER RESERVOIR
GREEN HOUSE
GROCER'S STORE
HABITATION

FLOOR LEVEL 1

N

bc2ff Industrial Garden House CH

| Szymon Banka | Architect | szy_ban@interia.pl |
| | EU_Poland | Silesian University of Technology in Gliwice |

Poverty and degradation of postindustrial areas are a region's main urbanization problems. **PHASE 1** The "green implant" resembles a plant seedling placed in the heavily eroded soil. It is supposed to heal the degraded environment. It is assumed that the "implant" structure will include: public areas (parks), semi-public grounds (like towers) and private terrains (living flats). **PHASE 2** Two extremities meet: the urbanized area (postindustrial landscape archetype) and the open green grounds (the country-like archetype). The overlapping of these archetypes yields the new typology of the family flat (industrial garden house). The industrial part (negative) is employed as a source of energy for the residential district. Energy could be generated for example by utilizing the few hundred feet tall chimneys, buried deep in the ground so that only the short upper parts are visible. The lower ends of the chimneys would reach down to the coalmine tunnels, where the air pressure is different than above the ground. This would generate the airflow, which could run current generators.

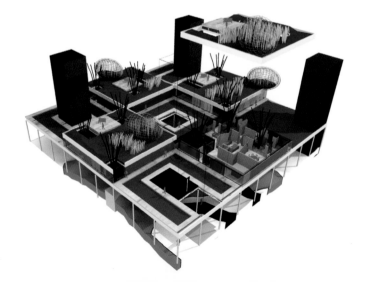

 NATURE SPACE

INDUSTRIAL NATURE
S P A C E

INDUSTRIAL
S P A C E

POSTINDUSTRIAL
S P A C E

GREEN IMPLANT
S P A C E

GARDEN + HOUSE = GARDEN HOUSE

 + =

GARDEN + INDUSTRIAL = INDUSTRIAL GARDEN

 + =

 + =

INDUSTRIAL GARDEN HOUSE

industrial garden
h a u s e

garden h a u s e

industrial garden

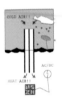

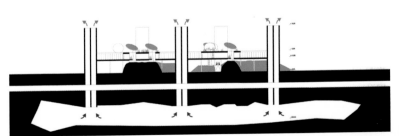

| —Yungbum Hahn, —Christoph Haerter | — Architect | — y.hahn@h2-architects.com |
| | — NA_USA | — H2 Architects |

The site chosen for developing self-sufficient and ecologically oriented collective dwellings is the Hudson River, just offshore of the Borough of Manhattan, between 61st and 68th Streets. The Hudson River (running 152 miles from the Federal Dam at Troy, New York down to the ocean, ending at the Battery in New York City) is one of the most ecologically significant tidal estuaries in the United States. Maintaining a balance between ecology and human use is one of the most important problems facing the future of our planet and the site was chosen for its ecological sensitivity, high population density and high profile. With the population of New York City at over 8 million, the proposal to develop sustainable housing on the Hudson River in New York City provides an opportunity for the adaptive reuse of New York's notoriously underdeveloped shoreline, provide much needed housing and educate millions of people about environmental awareness.

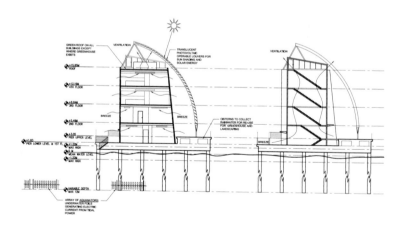

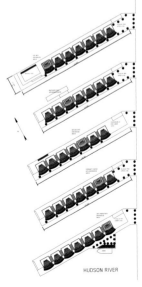

HUDSON RIVER

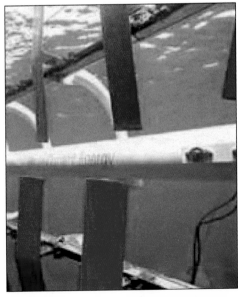

e3ada

Autarkical Genotype

| – James Brazil | – Student | – jimmy_b_au@yahoo.com |
| | – AC_Australia | – lab[RE] |

This project begins to formulate a response to the notion of a self-sufficient dwelling that seeks to explore a harmonious equilibrium of man-made and natural ecologies that are interwoven into the built environment by which they can be supported over time.

A miniaturized container of urban evolution is then explored through the development of a new generative collective building typology, a genotype for continual growth. The project accommodates and stimulates growth, much the same way that cell organisms multiply, continually expanding and contracting as social, economic and environmental relationships shift. The inherent strength of these organisms gave rise to a form that mirrors itself cross-axially, thus beginning to balance vertical and horizontal urbanism. The façade system continues this analogy to the landscape paradigm by creating an integrated 4D facade that moves in real time to wind movements, converting the kinetic energy of steel fins on the façade to an electric charge via piezoelectric cells.

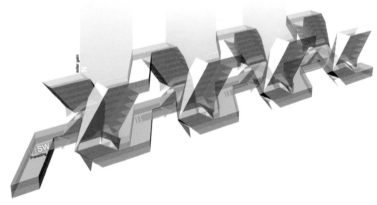

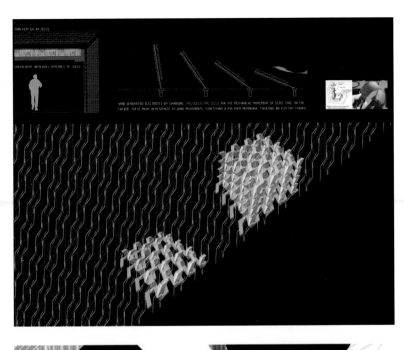

THIN FILM SOLAR CELLS

GREEN HUE INCREASES EFFICIENCY OF CELLS

WIND GENERATED ELECTRICITY BY CHARGING PIEZOELECTRIC CELLS VIA THE MECHANICAL MOVEMENT OF STEEL FINS. ON THE FACADE THESE MOVE IN RESPONSE TO WIND MOVEMENTS, STRETCHING A POLYMER MEMBRANE, CREATING AN ELECTRIC CHARGE.

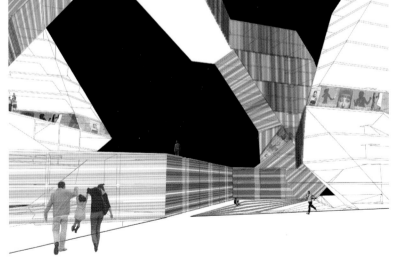

- Boguslaw Witkowski
- Marek Morawski

- Architect

- witkowski@skynet.be

- EU_Belgium

- Town Planning Design & Architecture

Revitalization of the former Tour & Taxi Station Area. We propose the creation of a concept based on a beehive pattern or an anthill rather than the modernist box or on high-tech morphology. The destroyed natural landscape should be restored and rebuilt with an architecture based on the interaction between vegetation of the surrounding installations (Royal Park of Laeken, navigation canal) and the newly created volumes. The soft and natural create tectonic lines that remind us that we are part of Nature, yearning for peace and harmony. If this vision, which resides outside the rigid frame of existing town planning regulations, does not correspond to your conception of the future image for human setting please stop your examination of our project! The hill-like structure will house various urban programs (cultural, sport, commercial, education, residential) with an important positive impact on the environmental quality.

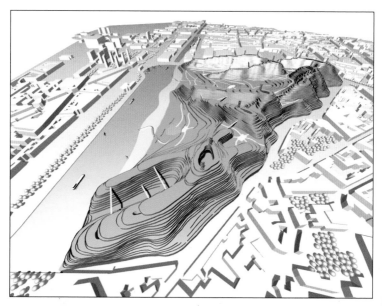

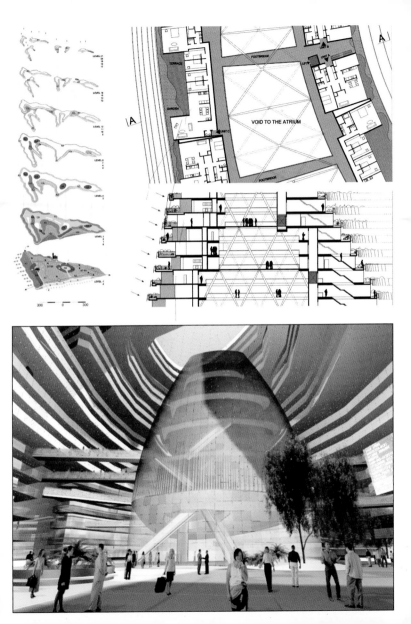

TERRACE

FOOTBRIDGE

GARDEN

UNIT C

VOID TO THE ATRIUM

FOOTBRIDGE

LEVEL 21

LEVEL 18

LEVEL 12

LEVEL 8

LEVEL 4

LEVEL 2

LEVEL -1

300   0   300

c6Se3	NoW_here City	SH

Alberto Javier García Martos	Architect	ak54@ya.com
Kira Pinedo Pérez	EU_Spain	ETSA Granada

The project is developed in the Natural Park of Sierra de Cazorla, Segura and Las Villas (PNCSV) the biggest natural park in the Iberian Peninsula. The strategy of the project consists of the creation of a multifunctional environment at the PNCSV. The proposal is a hybridization of the uses via the utilization of new technologies and the urbanization of the landscape. It makes good use of the global for the local development: the globalization of the PNCSV. With new technologies (wi-fi) it is possible to create a landscape in the net, a new balance between the environment and the new inhabitant. The nodes with a fractal development allow the development of connected communities and of forest control (collecting biomass). The new inhabitant has its own individual prefabricated kit of photovoltaic trees, rainwater tank and biomass, as well as an interface with the net: home and job. The wi-fi nodes are also the third places, where the possibility of relationships increase and are made physical.

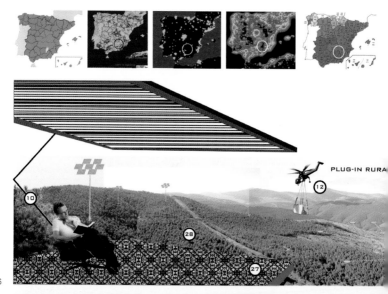

PLUG-IN RURA

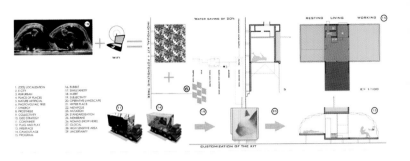

1. (DES) LOCALIZATION
2. E-CITY
3. RURURBAN
4. PLACE OF PLACES
5. NATURE ARTIFICIAL
6. PHOTOVOLTAIC TREE
7. SYNERGY
8. PROSTHESIS
9. COLLECTIVITY
10. GEO STRATEGY
11. CONTAINER
12. PLUG-AND-PLAY
13. INTERFACE
14. CAMOUFLAGE
15. PROGRAM
16. BUBBLE
17. SIMULTANEITY
18. INJERT
19. SUBJECTIVITY
20. OPERATIVE LANDSCAPE
21. HYPER PLACE
22. METAPOLIS
23. MUTATION
24. STANDARDISATION
25. MEMBRANE
26. NOMAD (NOW HERE)
27. GLOCAL
28. HIGH SENSITIVE AREA
29. UNCERTAINTY

WATER SAVING OF 20%

RESTING   LIVING   WORKING

CUSTOMIZATION OF THE KIT

WIFI

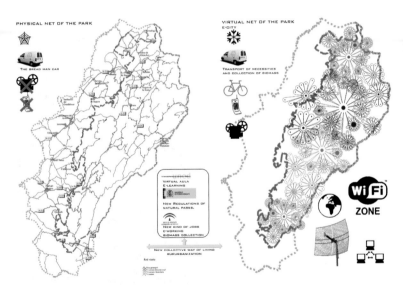

PHYSICAL NET OF THE PARK

THE BREAD MAN CAR

VIRTUAL AULA
E-LEARNING

New Regulations of
Natural Parks.

New Kind of Jobs
E-WORKING
BIOMASS COLLECTION

NEW COLLECTIVE WAY OF LIVING
RURURBANIZATION

VIRTUAL NET OF THE PARK
E-CITY

TRANSPORT OF NECESSITIES
AND COLLECTION OF BIOMASS

WiFi ZONE

2b523 Water Housing CH

- Giacomo Bongiorno
- Thomas Bormann
- Djamel Kara
- Bernard Ropa

- Architect

gcmbn@hotmail.com

- EU_Italy

- Politecnico di Milano

Experiencing the landscape of the plains surrounding the River Po was stunning especially in winter: fields of green glass stretching in all directions were at odds with the thick layers of snow; covering the neighboring suburbs of Milan. This integrated system is now regarded as a valuable natural ecosystem of unique richness. Despite official recognition and the establishment of parks, high costs of maintenance and lack of alternative policies make it difficult to keep those semi-natural oases alive.

Water housing exploits underground water for climatizing single family dwellings, organized in rows. Each house is a semi-autonomous element with a private underground patio and shared common energy system. Grouped in rows with a variable length, the water houses give form to a hybrid landscape that maximizes contact with farmland and nature. A new, low-density grid of low density melts into the landscape of the plain, offering an ecologically concerned alternative to the formless sprawl of the plain: an up-to-date version of the Prairie way of life.

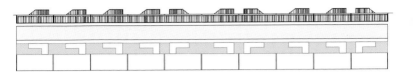

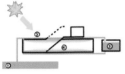

summer

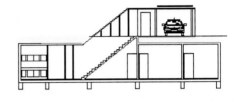

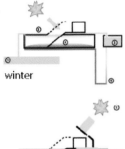

winter

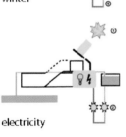

electricity

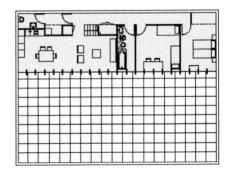

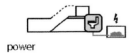

power

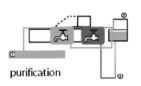

purification

- Carlos Enrique De Lima
- Student
- manoperro@gmail.com
- SA_Brazil
- Universidade de Brasília

THE WAY MATERIAL IS USED Solid residues produced in building construction are not entirely treated in many cases. Their impact on the environment is uncalculated, from extraction until final application. Thus, wood emerges as a material that has few production stages and whose possibilities have yet to be completely explored. The site of the collective dwelling is a forest-wielding area threatened by urban expansion. The wood structure pervades the collective spaces as a curtain that acts as both structure and enclosure. It also helps to support the plateaus, any one of which contains different kinds of wood species. On the highest level, there are water reservoir and wind-energy structures. There is also a green field of vegetables for consumption by the dwellers. **THE GRADATION OF COLLECTIVE AMBIANCE** A self-sufficient ambiance must be created not only through efficient energy use and the way materials are employed, but also through the potential to maintain the population of the dwellers on a long-term basis. In this case we explored the vaporization of collective areas. Thus, the self-sufficient housing attains a specific level of dialogue between nature, environment and man.

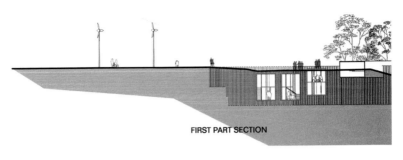

FIRST PART SECTION

8

Theory

Based on the successive phases of essay, hypothesis and pronouncement, Theory approaches rather than engaging with or practising the self-sufficient home from the viewpoint of the domain and the distance of critique and design.

From its genesis, at all times attending to a previous state, it actually reconsiders the most profound issues of the present-day city's mass housing that is closed, static and practically indifferent to worsening environmental factors. As a tool for thought rather than a direct solution, Theory covers a variety of scenarios, and its critical condition and conceptual stance give it a mobility that is less conditioned than practice. It is a reference generated by methods of analysis and investigation.

Some examples address the logics of emergency and aid. One such is Biloxi, a scenario

determined by the effects of Hurricane Katrina
in 2005, when the needs for sanitary conditions, water, shelter, food and security were
preceded by a shortage of resources, and the
disaster left the territory inherently damaged.
The self-sufficient dwelling, then, according
to Biloxi, should be prepared to provide post-
traumatic solutions to these situations.
And as it is not, it has to be reconfigured
from a series of containers and using waste
and remains left by the hurricane.
It came into being in this way, like a contin-
gency plan, like an emergency mechanism that
is also a drug that originates in the illness it
seeks to treat. Similarly, Korogocho, from the
rubbish a good prophecy, suggests that the
dwelling be self-sufficient principally in terms
of the optimum recycling of the refuse and
waste already produced in cities.

It is a type of building conceived as an entity that goes back to reuse the energy of the materials that it or someone else has rejected, as a by-product.

This is also a dwelling that is suitable for marginalized communities.

Fisher body 21 extends its critical approach to the very notion of self-sufficiency, positing that construction is a force governed by a single direction, the extraction of resources, which obviously has a high environmental price. By way of solution, firmly based in the field of theory, it posits a new class of economy-city-building that challenges the present-day process of industrial production by generating a second nature, an updated version of the interface between post-industrial construction process and inhabitants.

- Jason Pressgrove | - Architect | - nltlu@yahoo.com
| - NA_USA | - Mississippi State University, USA

CONTEXT: BILOXI, MISSISSIPPI When does sustainability matter? Today, Hurricane Katrina hit our shores. The wind and the water left very little standing in their massive, collective wake. When the wind finally calms, and the waters recede, we look around. We ask, what are the Needs? What are the assets, what do we have, what is of benefit, what do we know about living, about BEING ALIVE? The resources abound. There is material scattered and piled meters high all around. There are plastics and metals from a seemingly lost and forgotten world, the constructs of a civilization long gone and far removed. Modules of wood and waste to be reclaimed and put to a truly appropriate re-use. Mountains of "homes" to be excavated from the vast landfill we once knew as Biloxi. The hurricane has brought opportunity. And, only in our throat's thirst for water, can we SEE it.

CONTEXT: CRITICAL CONDITION: HURRICANE KATRINA

= Category 5 Hurricane

= Wind Speed - Upwards of 160 kilometers per hour

= Storm Water Surge -6 Meters

sail

building lumber

fiber-glass

metals

barrels

shipping containers

plastic sheathing

- Martin Assa
- Alexandra Verfaillie
- Sandrine Taillemite

- Architect

- martin.assa@wanadoo.fr

- EU_France

- EAPVS

Self-sufficient housing involves new and complex technologies, which, to be effective in terms of investment, maintenance, materials and implementation, must favor a collective approach.

We are committed to the establishment of a system favoring the emergence and survival of self-sufficient housing by establishing an enterprise (the S.C.H. Network) whose goal is the development, promotion, and management of a network of Self-Sufficient Collective Housing. Each dwelling will be designed according to its location by a team of specialists. The inhabitants will not be individually owners, but will be shareholders in the S.C.H. Network, their dividends a calculation of the function of the surface area of their dwelling, their projected energy consumption, and the local environment. Through their shares, which determine the distribution of available energy, the level of fees, and so on, the inhabitants will become partners in the enterprise. The personal lifestyle of each inhabitant will have a direct effect on the stability of the system, an intelligent partnership between inhabitants and housing that will result in improved efficacy.

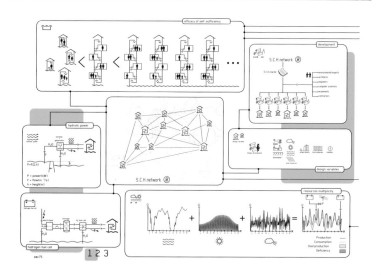

eac75

1 2 3

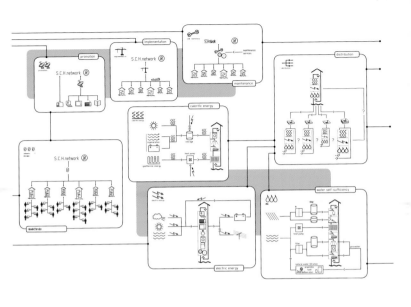

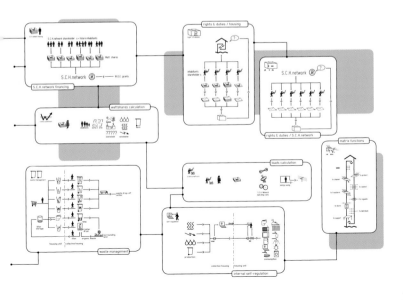

83aaS NEW re_CYCLE

–Frederic Reverseau –Andrea Curtoni	– Architect	– zoufred@hotmail.com
	– EU_France	– Ecole Du Breuil

Korogocho ("confusion" in the kikuyu language) is one of the shantytowns rising on the largest of Nairobi outlying dumping grounds. Here people live RE_using the "refused waste" of Mukuru, the waste-hill in front of Korogo-cho. Thanks to their work of the recovery and re_use of waste materials we have come to recognize these refusals as a source of energy.

We don't refer just to their thermoplastic value, but to the intrinsic material ability; the function of the object (can, bottle, packing...) is to be exhausted and not its material ability.

Cycling from extraction to consumption, from use to refuse, can be RE_cycled, where the end is a new beginning. We create circular modules made of materials extracted from the dump: plastics for living space, aluminium for structure and wood for common space. Around these common spaces, created by the relationship between the circular modules, communities organize their resistance to develop new ways of life.

21377   ? ...self-sufficient !!   SH

– Agustín Andre – Nicolás Newton – Gonzalo Parma	– Architect	– www.mu.com.uy – mu@mu.com.uy
	– SA_Uruguay	– Studio mu!!!

The true rationalization of the resources in the human habitat is achieved in the collective team, in infrastructures thought in an intelligent way for the metropolis. To think of SS_H in the present context is to think of housing in the city, inserted in the urban surrounding, taking advantage of the infra-structures and the existing facilities, the resources already invested and taking the best advantage of them all. For the SS_H today, its ecosystem is the metropolis, and its surrounding, urban.

The SS_H today, develops in the city. For the SS_H, sustainability is inter-action. Nature is also artificiality. Energy is information and technology. Development is recycling, reutilization. Thus, the space of the city begins to be perforated, becoming a continuous fluid. The urban space as a network of leaks (loopholes) and vectored spaces where an unexpected reality is strained, where free programs are developed, where the ways and prac-tices of the new citizen can be developed.

The final objective is the individual quality of life. The holes are a project in themselves... SS_H is The City for us; the equipment of our house, the urban equipment. We move inside it as if from bedroom to living room. Its borders are unknown for us. We share our house with our neighbors.

SS_H is The City for us; the equipment of our house, the urban equipment. We move inside it as if from bedroom to livingroom. Its borders are unknown for us. We share our house with our neighbours. Our house is The City and at the same time we, ourselves...

... Por eso nuestra SS_H es La Ciudad; el equipamiento de nuestra casa, el equipamiento urbano. Nos movemos dentro de ella como del dormitorio al living. No conocemos sus límites. Compartimos nuestra casa con los vecinos. Nuestra casa es La Ciudad y a la vez nosotros mismos...

SS_H resolves the demands of inhabiting in harmony with its environment. It fits the surrounding and lives on it.

SS_H administers the energy and the consumption of resources according to the circumstances.

"sabes que aquí, que allá, que en todos laos esta tu casa..." ("el Chole" Abuela Coca)

SS_H:

?...self sufficient !!!

| Chesney Gordon Floyd | Architect | mademanifest@gmail.com |
| | NA_USA | Berkeley College of Environmental Design |

Post-Industrial Detroit: The self-sufficient communities of today do not rise from a tabula-rasa, but are an evolution of industrial space. In order to explore the notion of self-sufficiency, we propose a new kind of building that treats the industrial city as a quarry. In addition to mining this 'second nature' for its embodied energy and latent geometries, we propose the re-introduction of stewardship and husbandry practices now forgotten in the urban landscape. The Fisher Body 21 project inhabits the old Fisher auto body plant. The design pursues two related agendas: 1– Selective reconstruction of the existing building in order to make it inhabitable, and to maximize the opportunities of its form, and 2– To introduce timber and wool harvesting in the surrounding lot (and the building itself). These agendas establish a logic of building, community and economy.

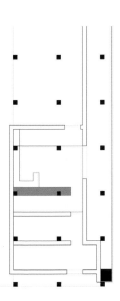

Daniel Georges	Architect	dani_georges@yahoo.com
	AS_Lebannon	ALBA, University of Balamand

Urban sprawl, in the form of developments on the outskirts of metropolitan hubs, has caused environmental destruction and tremendous increase of traffic and energy consumption, while failing to provide a convincing urban lifestyle of cultural and historical heritages.

The concept of the Space Vacuum is a theoretical spatial experiment exploring the vertical compressibility of space in a new type of mixed-use building. It is the direct architectural materialization of the adopted work model in urban society and a demonstration of its use as a means to reduce space consumption by deflating passive space and create more room for active space. Through the identification of a transferable height between oppositely operational functions like living and working, the concept allows a significant height cut-down of mixed-use buildings, reducing the natural resources consumption in the form of raw building material and lowering contribution to air pollution through a shorter construction time. Denser, greener and more attractive city life!

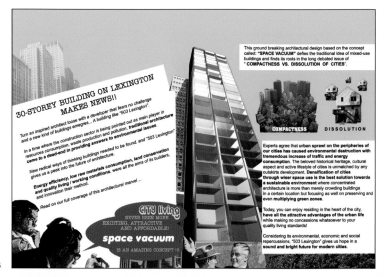

WHAT IS THE "SPACE VACUUM" CONCEPT?

Efficient space design defines the measurements of a certain room (office, bedroom, kitchen…etc) based on comfort, ease of circulation, the standard dimensions of furniture and appliances, thus allowing optimal conditions for the performance of a certain function in the least space possible.

Space efficiency has reached its limits on the horizontal dimension (unless beds disappear from bedrooms and desks from offices!) but huge space saving is still possible on the vertical dimension.

Since every function in a building has time-related operational periods, two new notions of height deriving from the regular notion of **Standard Height (SH)** can be identified:
Transferable Height (TH) and **Vacuum Height (VH)**, related as follows:

$$TH + VH = SH$$

The HOUSE model
- SH=3m — Based on: General standards
- VH=2.2m — Based on: Minimal height for operation and accessibility at anytime (24h)
- TH=0.8m

The OFFICE model
- SH=2.6m — Based on: General standards
- VH=1.8m — Based on: Minimal collapse height considering furniture and appliances (Desks, Computers, fixed low partitions…etc) Emergency accessibility only.
- TH=0.8m

OK, WHERE DOES THAT HELP EXACTLY?

The opposite operational time of the House and Office models allows the combined utilization of the two in one overall compact space in which their similar Transferable Height (TH=0.8m) will shift between the two by the means of a mobile light floor.

When the office is operational at its Standard Height (2.6m), the house is reduced to its Vacuum Height (2.2m), keeping it usable under medium comfort conditions. Usually the tenants will be outside at work or school during this time.

When the office is not operational, it shifts to its own Vacuum Height (1.8m) allowing the house to regain its optimal Standard Height (3m). The office will be only accessible in case of emergency.

The Vacuum period of a house will be dependent of the working hours of the office beneath it. These working hours will have limitations, the maximum time allowed could be the currently applied work break (9am to 5pm) or maybe a shorter work break (9am to 2pm), since the future foretells more work will be performed at home.

WOW! A MOBILE SLAB…

CARRY AWAY THE TECHNOLOGY FOR A REFRESHED LIFESTYLE!

PAST OR FUTURE?

SPACE VACUUM CONCEPT

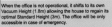

MMM, WHERE IS THAT BETTER THAN CONVENTIONAL DESIGN?

NOW… BEATING THE OLD SYSTEM !

The comparison between a conventional 30 stories mixed-use high rise and another based on the Space Vacuum concept reveals a **STAGGERING 18-20% cut down** on height for the same Living/Working floor space!

- 15stories living space — 3.4x15 = 51m — **48** **51**
- 15stories work space — 3.2x15 = 48m
- 30stories conventional mixed-use high rise — 48+51=99m — **99**
- 30stories Space vacuum mixed-use high rise — 5.4x15=81m — **81** **18**

Hundreds of tons of raw building materials can be saved, lowering our consumption of natural resources. Better preservation of of the environment will be possible due to shorter construction time! The reduced footprint of mixed-use building will allow more green areas to be planted on ground level !

IMPRESSING… CAN WE HAVE A CLOSER LOOK?

The inner quality of the building is accessible through the back circulation area containing independent elevators for apartments and offices, fire escapes…etc.

The typical floor plan is divided in modular units allowing maximum flexibility to merge the units and go from studio to apartment size or from small bureau to firm size dimensions.

Thick insulated separation walls contain the structure and shared technical components between living and workspace like heating and cooling systems (usually found in ceilings) enabling a light mobile slab.

Integrated multi-layers of sensors and cells control sun protection, insulation, daylight glare protection and ventilation in addition to passive and active solar energy usage.

The mobile aspect of the floors gives the building an ever-changing appearance at different points in time. Every time you look at it, the inner volumes are condensed or lit in a different way!
No high rise has better aesthetics!

FLEXIBLE HOME FOR A GROWING FAMILY

more GREEN spaces in the city for you and your friends to enjoy a day out!

CITY LIVING EXPENSIVE? THINK AGAIN…

Due to the same floor space provided by the Space Vacuum concept for a lower construction cost than traditional mixed-use buildings, developers promise rents will be **20%** lower than anywhere else in the city!

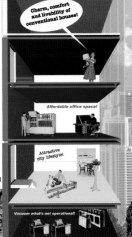

Charm, comfort and livability of conventional houses!

Affordable office space!

Attractive city lifestyle!

Vacuum what's not operational!

Wrapped

The self-sufficient home that is Wrapped is not expansive; rather it allows itself to be enveloped. Discreet, it can be covered totally or partially by a blanket of vegetation, by a portion of nature that covers it to produce a fertile, placid interconnection with it.

This action sees it fold back on itself to form an interior-exterior that is a heterogeneous surface with an open dynamic that blurs its limits to integrate it more smoothly into the environment.

This fold upon fold of vegetation, material, undulation and deformation of different strata of the territory constitutes the self-sufficient dwelling as an element that is shaped with the active collaboration of the landscape which, in turn, prompts processes of exchange within the ecosystem. In this way, the plant envelope offers highly efficient thermal control, at the same time providing many of the necessary elements for the water supply and removing the need for high maintenance required by more artificial approaches.

This is perhaps the taxonomy that is most attentive to environmental phenomena. The envelope proposed by Mutable changes substantially throughout the different periods of the year, causing the dwelling to alter even further in keeping with the yearly cycle.

The case of Temperate climate is similar, with formal relations that vary according to climatic change.

The Eko-kit, on the other hand, is more global in its application, responding to maps of biomass by reproducing the code that informs it. Depending on its location on the planet, the basic dwelling kit changes its configuration and adopts elements from its surroundings that readapt its systems, including elements for planting crops, collecting rainwater, regulating temperatures and even varying geometry to control sunlighting, producing a more efficient Clima-kit.

This configuration admits successive alterations indiscriminately, unlike the closed Spiruline system, with its semi-microscopic membrane of spirulina algae that envelopes the house like a greenhouse, covering the façade to activate the recycling of waste produced. The application of Wrapped, then, is associated more with non-urban environments and landscapes with a degree of human presence, and due consideration is given to its impact on the environment.

The common strategies are prudence and a high level of awareness of the chosen site, the ultimate aim being to leave it unaltered.

4c877 Inhabit climate

Carmen Anton Gamazo
Ana Gómez Cuesta

Architect — cmntg@yahoo.es

EU_Spain — ETSAM, Madrid

The interaction between natural materials (massive and energetically inert) and highly artificial materials (light and energetically active) are sensitive to the changes of their environment. This leads to composite systems in which the role of the natural is accumulative and reductive of exchanges and the role of the artificial is to generate and to attract energy resources. This technologically new model implies that the aspects of material organization shift to rational organization of consumed energy both in production and in maintenance of the built. Such a shift allows the consideration of current 'systems,' not just from the point of view of coherence and unity of materials, but also from their environmental coherence. In this way, the field opens to investigations in which the coherent mix of heterogeneous materials becomes a new and characteristic visual feature. A hybrid nature that involves a deep transformation of aesthetic ideals that adjusts with the racial mixture of our human landscapes.

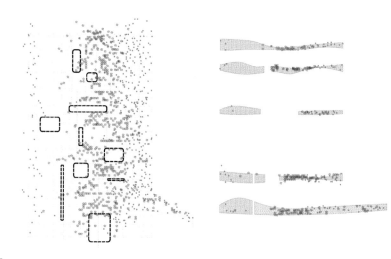

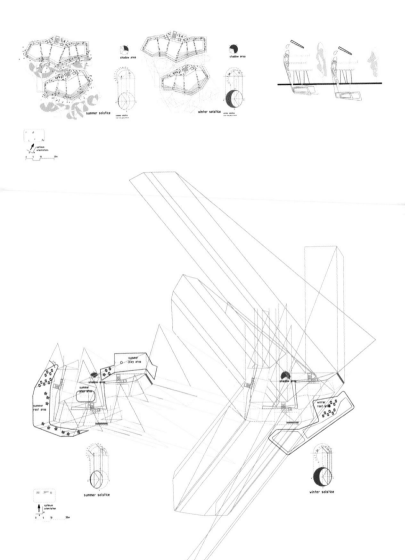

summer solstice

winter solstice

summer solstice

winter solstice

6fe96   Eko-media House   SH

-Bruno Vodan Juricic	- Architect	- www.met-7.com - juricic.bruno@gmail.com
	- EU_Croatia	- IUAV, Venezia

The bamboo growth process as a generative/sensor/data architecture project applied to natural structures: Bamboo comes in many colors, sizes, and textures. Bamboo is a grass that has many different species. Bamboo is the fastest growing plant. Bamboo charcoal (takesumi) has great absorption and decomposition ability, releases negative ions, emits infrared rays, shielding from electromagnetic radiation. In the project site we planted seeds of bamboo or young bamboo seedling distributed in relation to the program/function of the house. Placed over the so called "morphology body," a machine or "automat" constructed by a linear-actuator, ball joints, and metal bars, all modified in relation of output from sensor/computer systems that through an evolutionary software process manages the data from sensors. All this data affects the morphology body that functions as the data/driven support for the bamboo growth. This house project is no longer based on an optimization model but on an evolutionary algorithm that pushes the concept of sustainability

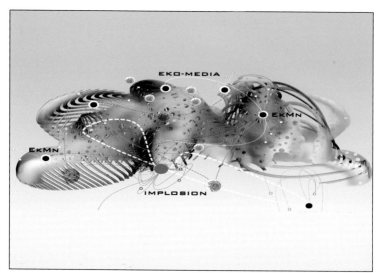

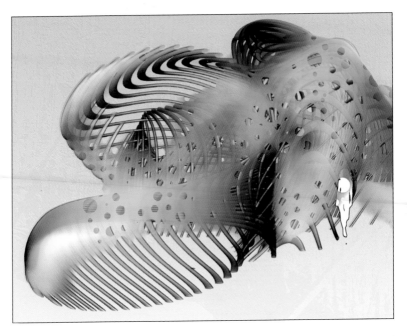

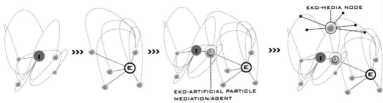

EKO-MEDIA NODE

EKO-ARTIFICIAL PARTICLE
MEDIATION/AGENT

SSdga	**Sun Deck**	**CH**

-Felix Sommerland -Michael Reiss	- Student	- sommereiss@gmx.net
	- EU_Germany	- Technical University Berlin

COLLECTIVE HOUSING, IN AND AMONG NATURE. The Sun Deck allows a lifestyle independent of conventional electricity and water supply systems. These important resources are supplied by a river, in conjunction with a water wheel. Up to ten single housing units on three floors are created by a scaffolding-type structure. The ground level functions as the public zone, the two upper levels as private areas. Green, living materials provide not only structural, but also decorative qualities. The housing units are constructed with timber frames and plants create a huge variety of outside spaces and interior qualities. The water wheel, in combination with a generator, guarantees the power supply. Potable and industrial water is extracted from a well with appropriate filters. Waste water is returned to the natural cycle on a seeping field. The inhabitants' versatility and their individual use of plants makes each little settlement of Sun Deck a unique specimen.

| –Pablo Muñoz
  Bahamonde
–Oscar Terrazas | –Architect– | –pablojmb@yahoo.es |
| | –SA_Chile | –Universidad Mayor, Chile |

In the routes of the 21st century, communications will take over the motor operations of the individual, reaching the point in which men will have to collect mutable data with the aim to favor our stay in this planet... a refuge able to receive climatic sensations of this new so-called "tele" information organism ("tele-world"). The house of this era should respond in an efficient way to the ecosystem where it is located and extract energies in order to maintain its operations. Like an animal who adapts to climatic conditions, through mutation, so its aspect transforms according to existing data. Eco-kit responds to an extensive database, taking into account the basic user survival requirements and extraction possibilities of optimal energies from the environment where it is inserted. An advanced way of understanding the current occupation of our planet, where information systems will be the base of our communities.

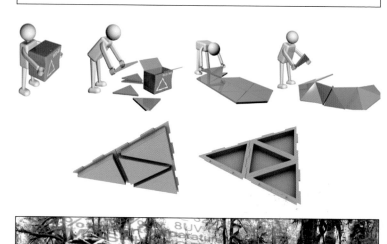

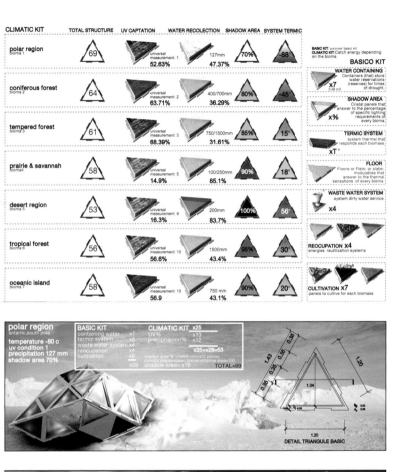

CLIMATIC KIT	TOTAL STRUCTURE	UV CAPTATION	WATER RECOLECTION	SHADOW AREA	SYSTEM TERMIC
polar region bioma 1	69	universal measurement: 1 — 52.63%	127mm — 47.37%	70%	-88°
coniferous forest bioma 2	64	universal measurement: 2 — 63.71%	400/700mm — 36.29%	80%	-45°
tempered forest bioma 3	61	universal measurement: 3 — 68.39%	750/1500mm — 31.61%	85%	15°
prairie & savannah bioma 4	58	universal measurement: 5 — 14.9%	100/250mm — 85.1%	90%	18°
desert region bioma 5	53	universal measurement: 9 — 16.3%	200mm — 83.7%	100%	56°
tropical forest bioma 6	56	universal measurement: 10 — 56.6%	1500mm — 43.4%	95%	30°
oceanic island bioma 7	58	universal measurement: 10 — 56.9	750 mm — 43.1%	90%	20°

BASIC KIT: survivor basic kit
CLIMATIC KIT: Catch energy depending on the bioma

BASICO KIT

WATER CONTAINING
Containers (that) store water reservations (reserves) for times of drought.
x7   0.48 m3

SHADOW AREA
Cristal panels that answer to the percentage of specific lighting requirements on every bioma.
x%

TERMIC SYSTEM
system thermal that responds each biomass.
xT°

FLOOR
Floors-or Flats- or slabs- modulables that answer to the thermal sensations of every bioma.

WASTE WATER SYSTEM
system dirty water service
x4

REOCUPATION x4
energies reutilization systems

CULTIVATION x7
panels to cultive for each biomass

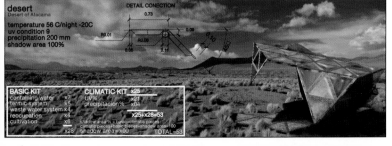

polar region
antartic,south pole

temperature -80 c
uv condition 1
precipitation 127 mm
shadow area 70%

BASIC KIT
containing water   x7
termic system   x5
waste water system   x4
reocupation   x4
cultivation   x6
                      x28

CLIMATIC KIT x25
UV%   x13
precipitacion%   x12
                 x25+x28=53
shadow area % = basic-climatic pieces
climatic pieces+basic pieces+shadow area=100
shadow area= x16   TOTAL=69

1.43   0.36   0.36   0.36   1.20
0.36   0.35
1.04
1.20
DETAIL TRIANGLE BASIC

desert
Desert of Atacama

temperature 56 C/night -20C
uv condition 9
precipitation 200 mm
shadow area 100%

DETAIL CONECTION
0.73
R0.01   R0.08
0.09   0.10   0.11
0.08

BASIC KIT
containing water   x7
termic system   x5
waste water system   x4
reocupation   x4
cultivation   x6
                      x28

CLIMATIC KIT x25
UV%   x21
precipitacion%   x04
                 x25+x28=53
shadow area % = basic-climatic pieces
climatic pieces+basic pieces+shadow area=100
shadow area= x00   TOTAL=53

33963 Housing in Athens CH

- Juliet Zindrou
- Xanthopoulos Pavlos
- Blazetti Ezio

- Architect

- EU_Greece

- www.otn.gr
- zindroujulia@yahoo.gr

- National Technical University of Athens

The research in sufficiency follows two directions: 1— SPACE Buildings provide changeable space, to satisfy alternate needs generated through time. 2— ENERGY Buildings produce the energy needed, without fuel cost or large equipment. The way that industry functions, by promoting mass customization, creates open fields of research concerning space and object identity, pointing out a new approach in the case of dwelling. The designed space-object satisfies the possible need for mutation through alteration. It is changeable and promotes recycling at the housing scale. The designed "garden-window" functions as a greenhouse: a combination of layers, as punched green-planted wall, water and glass, maintain favorable micro-clime in the interior. Researches in interactive materials pointed out a polymer (used for medical and industrial uses) which mutates its shape via changes in electron flow. The introduction of applicable equipment provide a mechanism that interacts with the environment and absorbs natural energy. Houses obtain muscles and lungs, becoming organisms. Deep inside the organism "house," lays an auto-poetic core that identifies itself every moment through chaotic intersections of various elements. This sense of the auto-poetic core and the element of nature are certainties.

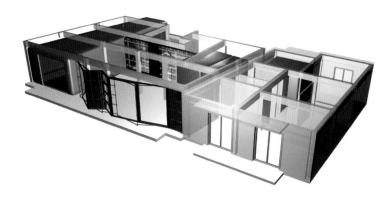

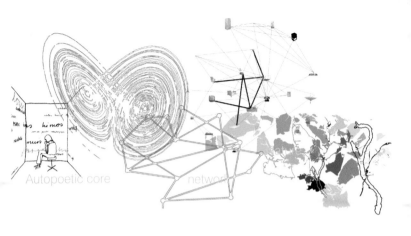

Autopoetic core network

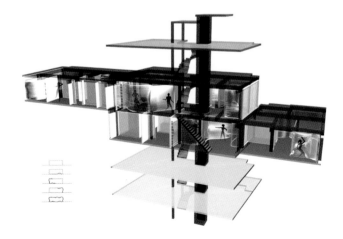

982b3 Spiruline House SH

Benoit Rougelot Didier Chéneau	Architect	http://landfabrik.free.fr landfabrik@free.fr
	EU_France	LANDFABRIK

ECOLOGICAL FOOTPRINT We propose a model of self-sufficient individual housing where inhabitants can be completely autonomous by producing their own energy and food. They need 0.08ha for 3 persons. (2720 kcal/person/day). The concept is shelter + food or house + garden (h+g)

200 m² provide 2 000 kg of vegetables (needs are 300kg/person/year)
200 m² provide 1 000 kg of cereal (needs are 100 kg/person/year)
domestic water represent 120L/person/day

SOME TECHNICAL SOLUTIONS Solar thermic panel provides hot water; storage heating pebbles keep warm in winter and cold in summer; photovoltaïc cells provide electricity; rainfall is stocked (150.000L); dry toilet spare 25% of domestic water amount and can be use to produce biogas (for cooking and heating) and compost; an oven placed in middle of house emits heat throughout the clay core (bathroom); uses of coppices (cultivated woodlands) for a bread oven and fruit drying area; rainfall for this area is 550mm, which is perfect for wheat cultivation.

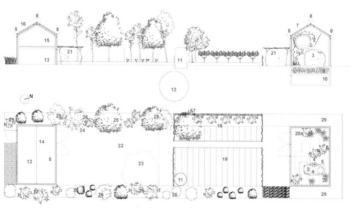

1.house
2.bedroom
3.bathroom (dry toilet, shower...)
   made of clay, glazed inside, natural outside
4.kitchen
5.oven
6.spiruline wall (double glazing)
7.thermic solar tube
8.ventilation
9.storage heating pebbles

10.methanization room
11.biogaz storage
12.rainfall storage (150.000L)
13.animal farm
14.storage (fire wood, tools...)
15.storage (hay...)
16.photovoltaic panels
17.stone wall (accumulate heat for fruit trees)
18.orchard (fig,pear,apple,cherry,orange...)
19.vegetable garden

20.aromatic garden
21.trellised vines+kiwi
22.cereal-oleaginate rotation culture
23.chicken enclosure on fallow field
24.compost
25.big tree (chestnut,oak,quince...)
26.thickets (hawthorn,hazel,raspberry,currant bush)
27.osier
28.protective hedge from wild animals and wind
29.grassland

64313 — A house is an organism — CH

- Mª Jesús Gonzalez Diaz
- Miguel Angel Romero Ramos

- Architect
- EU_Spain

- mjg@torredecomares.com
- ETSAM, Madrid

A house is not a machine, it is an organism. Likewise, the different levels of grouping are organisms: a block of houses, a large square, a district, the community and the town or city.

All these levels of grouping possess incoming and outgoing flows which require management. A house must obtain the balance between the incoming flows of a house (food, fuel for acclimatisation, water, consumer goods, newspapers, etc, should be managed in the same way as the outgoing flows) solid, recyclable and organic residue, pollution, stuffy air, and used consumer goods through adequate management. The idea is to remove the strict distinctions between country and town and eliminate the radical contradiction between those two. Other aspects, which have been considered as important in the project, are the sustainable city, its spatial configuration, its placement within nature, mobility, and material of low environmental impact, the strong influence of telecommunications, industrialisation, and the inclusion of functional "bio-diversity".

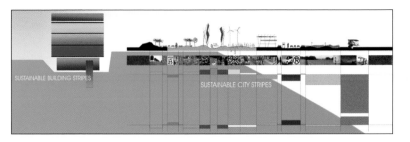

SUSTAINABLE BUILDING STRIPES

SUSTAINABLE CITY STRIPES

- Mohd Redza Abdul Rahman
- Mohd Daniel Iman bin Mohd Delan
- Ahmad Farihan bin Sudirman

- Student

- AS_Malaysia

- redrahman@yahoo.co.uk

Like the "Asplenium nidus" the house "grows" on the surface of the ground (host) without intruding much into the existing natural context. The parabolic roof of the house functions as a giant bowl that collects rain water to be filtered and piped for the use of the dweller. A ring of solar panels is installed along the inner rim of the parabolic roof to allow the accumulation of solar energy. 80 percent of the house is built using rubber, a product of latex, a processed natural protein serum. Latex is obtained from a special tree species known as the "Havea brasiliensis," which is grown in plantations all throughout Malaysia. It is one of Malaysia's important commodities and is therefore easily obtained for use. Although rubber has been known to produce various products, it has never been utilized as the main components for built materials. This project will also show how rubber can be exploited as a new building material that is efficient, cost-saving and sustainable.

| cb86c | Housing in Almería | | CH |

– Paul Galindo Pastre
– Ophélie Herranz Lespagnol

– Student

– EU_Spain

– paulgalindo80@hotmail.com

– ETSAM, Madrid

We believe there is a possibility to build an alternative dwelling type to accommodate the population of "El Ejido" immigrants. This model is different from the traditional urgency module and more adjusted to future dweller needs and to the specific Almerian environmental conditions. We propose the construction of 125 dwellings scattered across the greenhouses. The green interfaces receive the bioclimatic systems which are designed for each orientation and specific site parameters. The proposal looks for the maximum use of passive systems directly related to local conditions. With regard to heating and cooling, simple techniques are used to modify the building inside temperature by means of natural energy sources. In winter, thanks to the greenhouses and drum walls systems, there is warm air distribution and storage through the double envelopes. In summer, the greenhouses work as cooling systems: the warm air inside is extracted through the chimneys. Other passive systems are used: natural sun lighting systems; natural ventilation; dry garden landscaping; rainwater usage by communal collectors; moisture control; photovoltaic cells for energy supply.

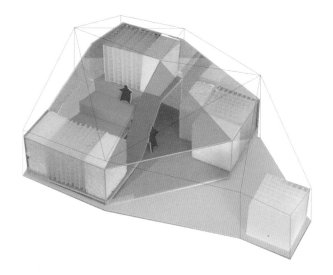

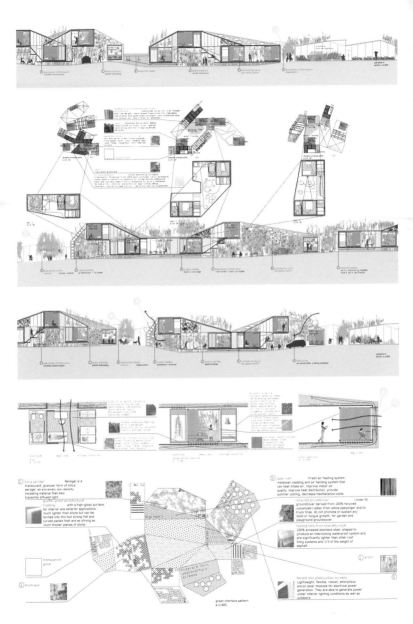

d46c8 Mecano - over 18 years SH

– Eberhard Schmidl – Mariaeva Sanchez	– Architect	– e_schmidl@lycos.at
	– EU_Austria	– TU Innsbruck

Imagine you live in a country, you have no infrastructure, you depend on basic elements and you don't have access to "high-tech" products like solar panels, heating or cooling systems. My definition of self-sufficient collective housing is the reduction of facility in production and transport, module systems, while maintaining the objective to create a new, "different" place of living. To recuperate resources, collecting energy is based on a basic process.

GEOGRAFIC SITUATION Senegal. **RESOURCES** 1– Water: collecting the quantity of strong rainfall and storing it in a well on the ground floor of the project. 2– Vegetative oil: circulating in black colored tubes to the roof and centered in the focus point of a lens, the oil warms easily. It will be used as cooking energy as well as part of electricity production. 3– Composting: collecting chopped vegetation / bio-trash of kitchen / grey water: being part a "catalysator" for the chemical process. 4– Plants: natural air-circulation, as well as giving shadow to the interior.

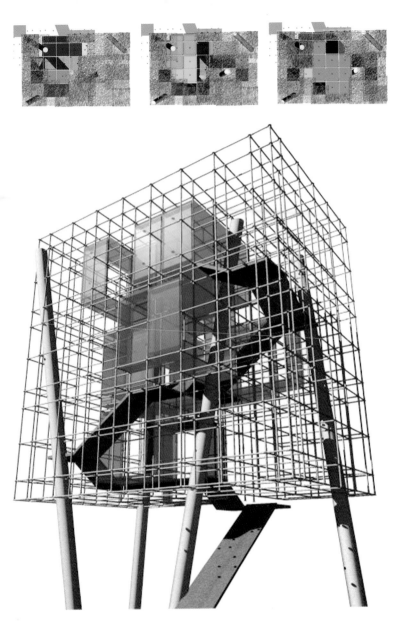

dd3f1 | Hydroponic Shelter | SH

−Alberto Tejada −Fernando Cucho	− Architect	− albertoricardo@hotmail.com
	− SA_Peru	− Rostov Architectural Institut, Russia

SUSTAINABILITY The project contemplates a positive impact in the economic future of the settlers by lodging hydroponic cultivations for self-supply and to commercialize the remaining products. The energy is reduced to a minimum while obtaining the construction materials, because these materials proliferate in the construction area. **FLEXIBILITY** The starting point is a zoning plan that responds to patterns of traditional uses. The use of the modular structure and of the interior "totora" (a typical Peruvian plant) membrane material system allows a high degree of flexibility. Thus, the membranes, tightened and anchored in the ground, serve as furniture for resting and socializing, as well as dividing partitions.

STRUCTURAL INNOVATION A flexible and interactive kinetic structure is formed by three dimensional cane modules that support the hydroponic cultivations. The union of several modules creates a flexible and moldable self-supporting weave able to adapt to different slopes.

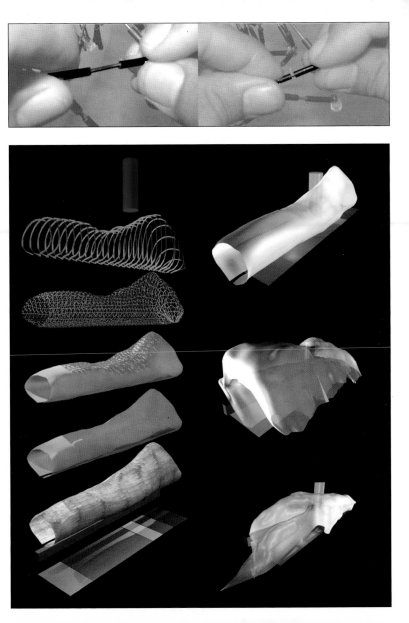

| –Hugo Dias
–Liliana Ferreira | – Student | – hugodias_arkitekt@hotmail.com |
| | – EU_Portugal | – Universidade de Évora, Portugal |

The form that best demonstrates purity, elementality and plasticity is the cube. A simple fragmentation of the cube generates a series of volumes that can correspond to the necessities of a contemporary habitat. A "play" of these volumes in the main cubic space generates expressive spatial variations allied to the tetra dimensionality, which allows ambiguities like interior/exterior, natural/artificial, equilibrium/instability, and light/materiality. This variation of the volumes are also a result of climatic issues and the owner can regulate two extreme positions: one with total use of the main cube and the volumes "expelled" and other with the volumes picked inside. The first for a better absorption of the sunlight in winter by the incorporation of photovoltaic cells in the exterior wood walls of the volumes. The second creates a labyrinth space protected by solar radiation. This idea is reinforced by the use of climbing vines, which not only mark the passage of time but also possess a plastic texture that adapts to necessities of isolation. There was also the preoccupation of the organic gathering of the vine leafs by a flower bed for its own renewal ability.

MASS DIVISION HALF MASS SPACE FRAGMENTATION EXPLOSION ORGANIZATION

−Calvin Chen	− Architect	− www.bcarc.com
−Thomas Bercy		powei@bcarc.com
−Thomas Lessel		
−Younglan Tsai	− NA_USA	− Bercy Chen Studio LLP

The concept for this house is to utilize rainwater and solar radiation together, through a heat engine and a heat pump, to obtain all the water and energy needs. Steam is expanded through a turbine to drive an electric generator and an air compressor, therefore eliminating any harmful pollutants. The structure is cubic, maximizing internal space to surface area. The structure consists of two parts: The inner core is a trussed tower supported in a spiral staircase; a water tank, held inside the tower, is used as a heat sink and a 20-day supply of water. The outer shell forms a greenhouse garden of hanging plants, providing food, shade, oxygen, and serenity. Ventilation is in a top-down cycle, were fresh air flows in under the roof to the core, and out at ground level. Air is moved by compressed-air powered ceiling fans, which also double as a sprinkler system, in case of fire.

SELF SUSTAINING HOUSE: PANEL 1

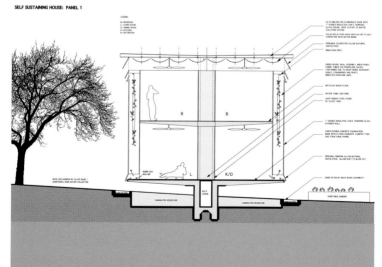

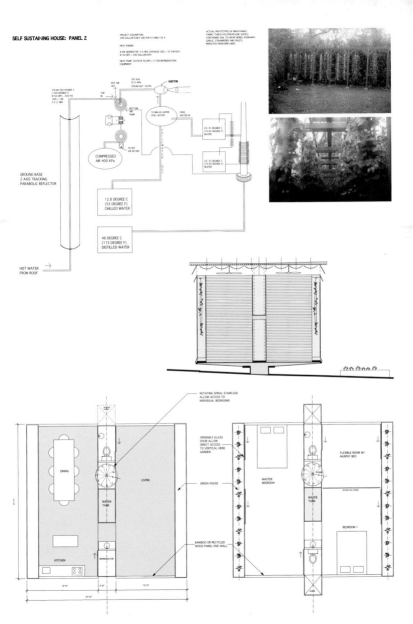

SELF SUSTAINING HOUSE: PANEL 2

d74dS Tree House

SH

| Daniel Moyano
Luis Batuecas
Santiago Cartón | Architect | dm@danielmoyano.net |
| | EU_Spain | ETSA Valladolid |

We pay special attention to the exploitation of natural resources, from water preservation to active and passive solar energy exploitation. The dwelling is located in north west Spain, in a town called Gijón. The self-sufficient single housing proposal is based on one of the most self-sufficient living beings, trees, without whom no human could live.

Trees are composed of three main parts: leaves, trunk and roots. Trees need five things to grow: light, water, nutrients, room to grow and well-drained soil. The most singular part of the Tree House is the 'trunk' and this is the way we will refer to the structural core of the house. The trunk is made of a thick concrete box and the stairs. Both components are surrounded by metallic pillars. The core of the house is inspired by the growth rings of a tree. Inside the 'trunk' are situated damp rooms of the house, required installations and the control boards of those installations. The joint of the structure, vertical communications and installations, liberates all the space around the trunk for the rooms.

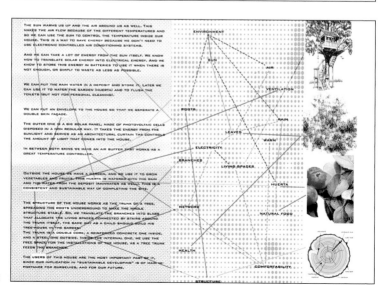

THE SUN WARMS US UP AND THE AIR AROUND US AS WELL. THIS MAKES THE AIR FLOW BECAUSE OF THE DIFFERENT TEMPERATURES AND SO WE CAN USE THE SUN TO CONTROL THE TEMPERATURE INSIDE OUR HOUSE. THIS IS A WAY TO SAVE ENERGY BECAUSE WE DON'T NEED TO USE ELECTRONIC CONTROLLED AIR CONDITIONING SYSTEMS.

AND WE CAN TAKE A LOT OF ENERGY FROM THE SUN ITSELF. WE KNOW HOW TO TRANSLATE SOLAR ENERGY INTO ELECTRICAL ENERGY, AND WE KNOW TO STORE THIS ENERGY IN BATTERIES TO USE IT WHEN THERE IS NOT ENOUGH, OR SIMPLY TO WASTE AS LESS AS POSSIBLE.

WE CAN PUT THE RAIN WATER IN A DEPOSIT AND STORE IT. LATER WE CAN USE IT TO WATER THE GARDEN (HUERTA) AND TO FLUSH THE TOILETS (BUT NOT FOR PERSONAL CLEANING).

WE CAN PUT AN ENVELOPE TO THE HOUSE SO THAT WE GENERATE A DOUBLE SKIN FAÇADE.

THE OUTER ONE IS A BIG SOLAR PANEL, MADE OF PHOTOVOLTAIC CELLS DISPOSED IN A NON REGULAR WAY. IT TAKES THE ENERGY FROM THE SUNLIGHT AND SERVES AS AN ARCHITECTURAL CURTAIN THA CONTROLS THE AMOUNT OF LIGHT THAT COMES INTO THE HOUSE.

IN BETWEEN BOTH SKINS WE HAVE AN AIR BUFFER THAT WORKS AS A GREAT TEMPERATURE CONTROLLER.

OUTSIDE THE HOUSE WE HAVE A GARDEN, AND WE USE IT TO GROW VEGETABLES AND FRUITS. THIS HUERTA IS WATERED WITH THE RAIN AND THE WATER FROM THE DEPOSIT (RAINWATER AS WELL). THIS IS A CONSISTENT AND SUSTAINABLE WAY OF COMPLETING THE BIKE.

THE STRUCTURE OF THE HOUSE WORKS AS THE TRUNK OF A TREE, SPREADING THE ROOTS UNDERGROUND TO MAKE THE WHOLE STRUCTURE STABLE. SO, WE TRANSLATE THE BRANCHES INTO SLABS THAT ALLOGATE THE LIVING SPACES CONNECTED BY STAIRS AROUND THE TRUNK ITSELF, THE SAME WAY AS A CHILD SHOULD BUILD HIS TREEHOUSE IN THE GARDEN.
THE TRUNK IS A DOUBLE CORE, A REINFORCED CONCRETE ONE INSIDE, AND A STEEL ONE OUTSIDE. INSIDE THE INTERNAL ONE, WE USE THE FREE SPACE FOR THE INSTALLATIONS OF THE HOUSE, AS A TREE TRUNK FEEDS THE BRANCHES.

THE USERS OF THIS HOUSE ARE THE MOST IMPORTANT PART OF IT, SINCE OUR IMPLICATION IN "SUSTAINABLE DEVELOPING" IS OF MAIN IMPORTANCE FOR OURSELVES, AND FOR OUR FUTURE.

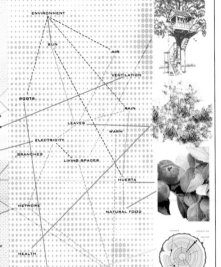

Participants

ID code	Name - Country
001f2	Tran, Joseph Nguyen - USA
00da3	Salihi, Alan Abdulkader - Libya
01d10	Garcia, Ma. Luisa Daya - The Philippines
01d27	Silberschneider, Eva Maria - Austria
02396	Abudajaja, Muftah Salih - Libya
02a84	Ferrer Piñeiro, Julio Cesar - Venezuela
0343f	Mulle, Felix - France
03a70	Sanchez-valladares, Xavier - Mexico
03af2	Beacom, Jesse - USA
049bf	Millán, Pablo Manuel - Spain
04dd0	Trongchittham, Vudthinant - Australia
053e2	Merone, Olindo - Italy
057a4	Utomo, Widianto - Indonesia
0583d	Chomali, Jonathan Alejandro - Chile
0601c	Arguello Santander, Juan Mauricio - Colombia
062a5	Haw, Alex Toby - UK
06d47	Bojanowska, Jowita - Spain
06dca	Tondo, Robert Joseph - USA
07875	Leblanc, Lisa Hassannati – Dominican West Indies
080cd	Umaña, Beatriz - Mexico
0836d	Bradecki, Tomasz Andrzej - Poland
08b7f	Fleming, Joy-anne Frances Josephine - UK
08c2c	Bechis, Nicolás - Argentina
09409	Larina, Katya Anatolyevna - Russia
09596	Young, Tan Jack - Singapore
09848	Olson, Mark - USA
0987a	Tattoli, Christian - Italy
09a26	Morais, Pedro Henrique Almeida De - Brazil
09a3a	Benites Fiusa Lima, Luciano - Uruguay
09aee	Nixon, Fiona - Australia
0a146	Maurer, Bernhard - Austria
0aa06	Nourrigat, Elodie - France
0ad02	Carbone, Carlo - Canada
0bda1	Hernandez Galvan, Luis - Mexico
0c91f	Olguín, Andrea Alejandra - Chile
0ce83	Torres, Alberto - Mexico
0de13	Van De Water, Charlotte - Netherlands
0e184	Kang-rang, Kompai - Thailand
0e724	Rovira Raurell, Esther - Spain
0f670	Amara, Andrew - Uganda
11096	Skowronska, Jolanta Skowronska - Poland
111f5	Kittsarakul, Pimwaree - Thailand

117a4	Ortega, Gonzalo Ignacio - Chile
12178	Gutierrez Patarroyo, Ricardo – Colombia
12779	Parid Wardi - Malaysia
134c6	Tinney, Sonja - Germany
13d77	Bougiatioti, Flora–maria - Greece
13d8e	Cuock, Juan Carlos - Mexico
14377	Gutierrez, Aaron - USA
144de	Armas, Jose Osvaldo - Argentina
15019	Schieda, Alejandro - Argentina
153f4	Grunninger, Courtney Johnston - USA
162b2	Conti, Anna Maria - Italy
17382	Divekar, Dnyanesh Vijay - India
178e4	Chan, Yi Mei - Canada
17b2d	Sintini, Matteo - Italy
18f73	Narutis, Lukas - Lithuania
19207	Cao, Yu - China
193e6	Wagner, Daniele - Italy
19840	Stiperski, Eva - Croatia
19a8a	Heacox, Mike - USA
19c6e	Sosa, Marco Vinicio - UK
19dec	Smith, Matthew - USA
1a4b4	Uenoyama, Takashi - Japan
1bd04	Zara, Enrico - Italy
1c6c2	Weiland, Shawn Matthew - USA
1c9c0	Papaefthimiou, Nicholas Demetrios - USA
1d718	Tortora, Giulia - Italy
1da64	Ivanescu, Emil - Rumania
1e2e7	Adrian, Tira - Rumania
1f4e7	Papadimitriou, Spiros Ioannis - Greece
20a96	Rubies, Gaston - Argentina
20ca9	Rivas Kubler, Carlos Daniel - Peru
21180	Beyer, Jörg - Germany
21377	André, Agustin - Uruguay
21b28	Martinez, María Del Carmen - Mexico
224b8	Bhattarai, Debesh Raj - Nepal
224f2	Smith, Jacqueline Jean - USA
229d4	Solanki, Kalpesh Ramesh - India
229db	Ruiz, Lionel To - The Philippines
22a63	Artemis, Fradelou - Greece
22ba5	Yamamoto, Junko - Japan
22c53	Daouti, Styliani - Greece
22f8d	Vranken, Lode – Belgium
24d8c	Voss, Yvonne - Germany
25b36	Gutierrez y Guerrero, Jonathan - Mexico
25e9c	Gallegos Isaziga, Gabriel Ignacio - Colombia
25ed5	Kawase, Chiaki - Japan
27053	Pedersen, Robert James - Australia
2731e	Riedel, William Christy - USA
276bd	Robles, Jesus Edmundo - USA

27aa5	Xie, Rujun - China
288ad	Muñoz Bahamonde, Pablo Javier - Chile
2981f	Bento, Pedro Duarte - Portugal
2aca4	González, Marinka - Mexico
2b523	Bongiorno, Giacomo - Italy
2b6d6	Rees, Joanna Roslyn - Australia
2bd44	Abelleyro, Fernando Gabriel - Argentina
2be10	Martino, Emanuele - Italy
2c028	Gaitan, Carlos Leopoldo - Venezuela
2c35a	Park, Sung Yong - South Korea
2c36a	Dominguez, Julio - Mexico
2c514	Twose, Pablo - Spain
2cd1e	Hariharan, Shilesh – India
2d05c	Dias, Hugo - Portugal
2dd76	Armstrong, Alan Paul - USA
2de55	Rivera Indarte, Marcos Ivan - Argentina
2ec79	Baaklini, Rabih Georges - Lebanon
2f20d	Konstantinovic, Dragana - Serbia & Montenegro
2f6de	Lamm, Carin Maria - Germany
2fc6a	Piriyaprakob, Nutthawut - Thailand
2fc9f	Stanic, Marko - Bosnia
2ff3f	Muthu, Sackthi - India
305c4	Geroulis, Michael - USA
3070c	Ben Shoshan, Hanan - Israel
3086b	Cuevas, Lucas Raul - Argentina
30a15	Sabu, Francis - India
311cd	Ledda, Antonio Maria - Italy
3132b	Ampuero, Javier Alejandro – Chile
31d99	Castilla Ibarra, Ana Luisa - Mexico
32a28	Aghazadeh, Bijan - Iran
32eba	Martin, Rodolphe - France
3366c	Garcia–badell, Guillermo Delibes - Spain
3389c	Union, Alexandra Audrey - France
339b3	Zindrou, Juliet – Greece
33a88	Jalilian, Louise - Sweden
34894	Hemmerle , Julie - France
34b31	Islam, Khandoker Tariqul - Bangladesh
350a0	Zaldivar Armenta, Ricardo - Mexico
35462	Floyd, Chesney Gordon - USA
3685c	Requejo, Roberto - Spain
36baf	Padua Campos, Eunice - Mexico
377ba	Kosmopoulos, Panos Ioannis - Greece
3b0f4	Gruber, Ernst - Austria
3b136	Khoury, Danny Romanos - Lebanon
3b524	Giussani, Elena - Italy
3b9d9	Cluzel, Gregory Calixte - France
3bbee	Davidson, Bryn , Australia
3dcb8	Lara, Alberto Braulio - Mexico
3dff0	Zacek, Tomas - Slovakia

3e23e	Vernet, David - France
3eaa9	Kim, Martin - Germany
3f1cb	Cervantes, Karen - Mexico
3f6d8	Khabazi, Mohamad - Iran
3fa1f	Mikolajczyk, Damien - France
404b3	Webb, Derrick Eugene - USA
40aaa	Aceves, Santiago - USA
40f7a	Tangalidou, Genovefa Heleni - Greece
417f8	Cañaveras Armero, David - Spain
41abb	Marques, Alberto Paulo - Portugal
42298	Englisch, Markus - Germany
42c0a	Warsi, Tahsinur Rahman - India
4327e	Meyer, Godfroy Yves – France
43ca4	García Ramírez, Luis Carlos - Chile
43f30	Fitzgerald, Colin Clark - USA
44fab	Sanchez, Walter Alberto – Argentina
46bb8	Trejo, Marco - Mexico
48709	Kouakou, Nanan - Togo
48a4f	Soon, Yean Tying - Malaysia
48f34	Zavala, Marisol - Mexico
49317	Mattheus, Sebastian Cristian - Argentina
49327	Teng, Quan Zhin - Malaysia
4b207	Doolittle, Joshua Hartwell - USA
4b64c	Fegali, Angelo - Colombia
4c364	Colorado, Juan Carlos - Mexico
4c5dc	Hwang, Hui-jin Kabbi - USA
4c877	Antón Gamazo, Carmen - Spain
4cba8	Malamuceanu, Roland - France
4d87e	Hernandez, Juliet - USA
4d99e	Marco, Gregori - Italy
4dcd3	Kiss - Miller, Katia - Brazil
4e349	Smith, Nic John - USA
4e431	Bertrand, Flavien - France
4e6f1	Hassouri, Avine - Iran
4ec4f	Maestre, Jaime Fernando - Colombia
5075a	Devi, Renuka - India
509e1	Escobar Doren, Irene Paulina - Chile
5125a	Heaviland, Mark Daniel - USA
521d9	Lamy, Cyril - France
527cd	Arandia, Ricardo - Mexico
53265	Eldefrawy, Sarah Hamed - Egypt
53c20	Chia, Tien San - Malaysia
53f43	Barbera, Massimo - Italy
53fb8	Nechiporchik, Andrew - USA
54510	Opperer, Christoph - Austria
54bce	Puerta Montalván, Javier Eliseo - Peru
55d9a	Sommerlad, Felix - Germany
56f5e	Gibson, Michael David - USA
5709c	Schwarzkopf, Jessyca - USA

5714e	Chhatwal, Anjit - India
576c7	Sistik, Michal Bombolo – Slovakia
57e29	Boonmee, Lalida - Thailand
57ec6	Scialpi, Carla Maria - Italy
5830b	Assis Machado, Rodolfo Francisco - Portugal
58c9a	Golik, Konrad Zbigniew - USA
59b6a	Rodrigues, Joana Sampaio - Portugal
5a2b7	Young, Laura - USA
5a53c	Carbonara, Claudia - Italy
5ad01	Salinas, Diego Rivera - Chile
5b260	Gigena, Cesar Gabriel – Argentina
5b98f	Craddock, Nigel John - UK
5bad8	Ruarte, Lucas Martin – Argentina
5c65b	Emili, Anna Rita - Italy
5d3ee	Khanna, Paras - India
5df64	Soto, Jorge Alberto - Mexico
5e105	Lasa Zingui, Gaylor - France
60033	Dawn, Adelaide - USA
60299	Quinn, Patrick Ryan - USA
613d3	Santos, Teresa Plácido - Portugal
62ffa	Sellamen Garzon, Fabian Camilo - Colombia
63101	Aretz, Laura Susana - Argentina
632fe	Ramos, Viktor Paul - USA
64313	González Díaz, María Jesús - Spain
65190	Rassel, Asaduzzaman - Bangladesh
653e0	Hermiz, Faris Joseph - USA
661d6	Sepici, Selin - Turkey
67121	Mañalac, Arthur Perez - The Philippines
67af0	Ayala, Christian Jose - USA
67e1c	Aldrighi, Luca - Italy
695c5	Ngan, Fung Ling - Hong Kong
6b8fe	Mallya, Sadashiv - India
6ceca	Lim, Joseph Ee Man - Singapore
6e021	Shuttleworth, Nathan Todd - Canada
6ecb7	Tong, Roderick Wai Hung - UK
6eef5	Valdés Navarro, Ana Gabriela - Mexico
6f4fe	Zivkovich, Shelley - USA
6f5f6	Chen, Calvin Powei - USA
6fe96	Juricic, Bruno Vodan - Croatia
70760	Drummond, Christopher Stuart - UK
709c0	Roth, Curtis Allen - USA
713fe	Mortada, Amr Amed - Egypt
723a6	Rosas, Guarda Joaquin - Chile
733f1	Alcocer, Rogelio - Mexico
73f6d	Giannotti, Emanuel - Italy
745e9	Ramos Pérez, Jorge - Spain
74e33	Ramos, Jorge Enrique - Cuba
757a7	Larionova, Ekaterina - Russia
75eac	Assa, Martin - France

76506	Bentancor, Luis Gualberto - Uruguay
76d40	Püschel, Jörg - Germany
76e46	Cornejo, Olga Arellano - Mexico
77337	Marcet, Jaume Nogues - Spain
79807	Badita, Liana Magda - Rumania
79c91	Mickey, Elizabeth Ann - USA
7c923	Larralde, Daniel Del Solar - Spain
7d651	Wilmore, Francis Earl - USA
7d67e	De Lima, Carlos Henrique Magalhães - Brazil
7d82e	Pressgrove, D. Jason - USA
7d97f	Krithivasan, Pavithra - India
7e6cc	Kohler, Gaetan - France
7e885	Williams, Nathan John - USA
7f314	Hirota, Eitaro - Canada
7f3d8	Baudoin, Luis Facundo - Venezuela
8073f	Moulin, Laurent - France
80930	Smith, Raymond - South Africa
821d7	Berenz, Todd Andrew - USA
83603	Vegliris, Grigorios Emmanouil - Greece
83a3c	Ibañez Moreno, Daniel - Spain
83aa5	Reverseau, Frédéric - France
84399	Carcamo, Oscar Alvarez - Chile
84809	Bien, Magdalena Lidia - Poland
8485e	Cruz, Gonzalo - Peru
8492a	Ohnishi, Yoko - Japan
8505d	Tan, Samuel - Australia
8596b	Capati, Alessandro - Italy
85c7c	Delfino, Federico - Italy
85ff6	Jeria, Yerko - Chile
86059	Chaudhry, Bindiya - India
881be	Meena, Nattira - Thailand
88cbc	Prakash, Anand - India
89bb7	Cianchelli, Liano - Argentina
8a77c	Zola, Zoka - Croatia
8b29c	Laviolle, Noémie Laure - France
8b8db	Djermanovic, Predrag Vlado – Serbia & Montenegro
8c2dd	Ecer, Ayla - Turkey
8ce48	Galvagni, Flavio - Italy
8d411	Aureli, Dario - Italy
8e51e	Wong, Matt - UK
8f6fa	Mack, Casey - USA
8f9e3	Toh, Hua Jack - Singapore
8fd21	Poochomsri, Sooksan - Thailand
902f0	Llobell Borrull, Jordi - Spain
90eed	Testolini, Pablo Angel - Italy
91296	Gourdoukis, Dimitris - Greece
91df8	Mabrouk, Islam Ahmed - Egypt
928e1	Wiscombe, Tom Warren - USA
9296e	Mahmood, Uthra - India

93086	Menard, Raphael - France
93daa	Wang, John Rodolfo - USA
9419d	Ghania, Gourrini - Algeria
94c39	Pacheco, Ana Gabriela Nolasco - Mexico
951d2	Iravani, Houtan - Iran
9555e	Pérez Paredes, Iván Basilio - Mexico
9629e	Wang, Peng - China
96d5a	Mellberg, Andreas - Sweden
981cd	Devi, Cindrela– India
982b3	Rougelot, Benoit - France
985f9	Pérez, Miguel Angel - Chile
9886c	Toole, Dan - USA
98a41	Catone, George - USA
993d2	Espinosa, Rychiee Lynn - USA
9b04e	Pedersen, Kent - Denmark
9b179	Natsume, Hideyuki - Japan
9bca5	Michael, Emilios - Greece
9bd20	Barril, Andrea Veronica - Chile
9ce2c	Gainza, Joseba - Spain
9d02e	Contreras, Daniel Silvestre - Venezuela
9d8d8	Velasco, Pamela Debora - Bolivia
9d946	Sarwat, Ahmed Syed - Pakistan
9da38	Martinez Rodriguez, Jose Manuel - Spain
9dd7b	Ellis, Sean Timothy - USA
9e19b	Montes, Tonatiuh - Mexico
9e94b	Jacquot, Julien Claude - France
9e980	Dayabhai, Ishwar - USA
9ecaf	Ojo, Ayodeji Olanrewaju - Nigeria
9f219	Carrizo, Maria Fernanda - Argentina
9f72d	Esquivel Guadarrama, Juan Carlos - Mexico
9fb36	Bigano, Carolina - Argentina
9ff4d	Moore, Ashley - USA
a1204	Van Loenhout, Rop– Netherlands
a127e	Abdul Rahman, Mohd Redza - Malaysia
a2952	Feigelson, Mathieu - France
a37ec	Brown, Daniel John – Australia
a41ea	Buckley, Nicolas - Peru
a41fa	Donoso, David Eduardo - Chile
a4725	Ma, Lisa - USA
a519f	Refalian, Ghazal - Iran
a53c7	Garba, Fareh - Nigeria
a5c11	Pazzaglini, Lapo - Italy
a6116	Marsico, Paolo - Italy
a6123	Royer, Adrien - France
a639c	Prata, Ricardo - Portugal
a7cf2	Brouillard, Olivier - France
a7edc	Coulanges, Aurélien - France
a84b8	Huertas Tafur, Felipe – Colombia
a8789	Ghassempoor, Amir - Iran

a9f31	Dauwe, Raf – Belgium
aa6ad	Nasti, Tommaso - Italy
ab34d	Vargas Moya, Michael Gerhard - Peru
ab55f	Boto, Hélio Miguel Pargana - Portugal
ab9c8	Smith, Eric Robert - USA
ac2fa	Rastorguev, Simon Vasilievich - Russia
acffa	González López, May Ling Beatriz - Venezuela
adb16	Ruali, Luca - Italy
ae975	Boyan, Antonio Sanchez - Bolivia
aec13	Gopalan, Manu Madhavan - India
aee60	Malan, Martin Ignacio - Uruguay
aeede	Kim, Hong Il – South Korea
af3b8	Weclawski, Lukasz Jan - Poland
afcbf	Ramirez Fernandez, Vera Esperanza - Mexico
b01e8	Porter, Ted Trussell - USA
b067b	Gonzalez Ruiz De Zárate, Manuel - Cuba
b0eed	Georges, Daniel Elias - Lebanon
b1365	Chiku, Yusei - Colombia
b1a71	Sanchez Roman, Felipe - México
b1f63	Crisp, Liz - UK
b2093	Sin, David Hyun - USA
b33b6	Faus, Pau - Spain
b37ec	Baudoin, Luis Facundo - Venezuela
b394d	Fraga, Rosa M Escudero - Spain
b39dc	Tang, Susan Fan-ju - Canada
b4f45	Castagno, Tania - Italy
b5531	Adhikari, Rabindra - Nepal
b5764	Galeazzi, Carolina Hartmann - Brazil
b579d	Costamagna, Erik - Italy
b63d1	Heizmann, Oliver - Germany
b67de	Caso Donadei, Rebeca - Spain
b6c89	Harland, Tim - Australia
b74ef	Triana, Natalia - Colombia
b77b5	Canessa, Nicola Valentino - Italy
b8fbd	Amitay, Erez - Israel
b966e	Guedes, Ricardo - Portugal
ba111	Solh, Omar - Canada
ba335	Gamas, Alejandro Antonio - Mexico
ba647	Bittorf, Antje - Germany
ba6f4	Chang-in, Teeradech - Thailand
baedf	Fiori, Paolo - Italy
bbd40	Varela Fernandez, Esteban - Uruguay
bc2ff	Banka, Szymon - Poland
bce7c	Aguilar Leon, Bernardo - Peru
bd783	Anderson, Laura Lee - USA
bd8ba	Ben Torres, Aleshiang - Dominican Republic
bdadb	Igunza, Alex Adagala - Kenya
be3ad	Fernandez, Ana - Sweden
bfceb	Lemiesz, Christian - Germany

bff90	Dauria, Carlos Agustin - Argentina
c056e	Hahn, Yungbum - USA
c07ed	Strunk, Nina - Germany
c0bf0	Paniagua, Silvana Tufinio - Mexico
c10f7	Vink, Jacques – Netherlands
c1483	Basarir, Lale - Turkey
c18b3	Racolta, Claudiu Constantin - USA
c2884	Betzler, Florian Stefan - Germany
c39ea	Usua, Mkpouto Akaninyene - Nigeria
c46e1	Herrera, Juan Carlos - Chile
c5ec4	Kurokawa, Motonobu - Japan
c65e3	García Martos, Alberto Javier - Spain
c68e8	Heacox, Annette Elisabeth - France
c6a7d	Brittain, Peter Ian - UK
c7457	He, Brick - China
c74e4	Nejur, Andrei - Rumania
c76be	Mann, Adam Broas - USA
c8c30	Kumyol, Buke - Turkey
c92aa	Lee, Tracy - Canada
c9a01	Koch, David Christian - USA
c9a5a	Ortiz Tejeda, Guillermo - Mexico
ca28e	Purcell, Aimee Renee - Usa
ca359	Pidcock, Caroline - Australia
ca359	Pidcock , Caroline - Australia
cabec	Radicini, Fabio - Italy
cb86c	Galindo Pastre, Paul - Spain
cc23c	Garber, Richard Jon - USA
ccbed	Videla, Pablo Martin - Argentina
cdff1	Smith, Graham John - Canada
cf693	Woods, Timothy Joseph - USA
cf7cd	Glab, Andrzej Wladyslaw - Poland
d027e	Dietz, Sebastian Carlos - Argentina
d18f5	Scarpinato, Marco - Italy
d218e	Nashiv, Ari - Israel
d22e5	Garrett, Brandon - USA
d2a66	Ault, Nicholas Wade - USA
d337e	Aldama, Sergio Andres - Uruguay
d34e6	Gonzalez Aleman, Carlos Antonio - Spain
d46c8	Schmidl, Eberhard - Austria
d4b8f	Sierra, Francesly - USA
d4fab	Purushothaman, Seejo - India
d52a6	Ghlichkhani, Hassan - Iran
d6bc5	Krunic, Dina – Serbia & Montenegro
d701a	Páez, Israel - Spain
d70ff	Williamson, Chris - UK
d74d5	Moyano, Daniel - Spain
d79db	Stefopoulou, Katerina - Greece
d7bca	Farfan, Ana Francis - Mexico
d8083	Bravo Wood, Claudio Andrés - Chile

d8d9c	Girón Zúñiga, Pablo Ignacio - Chile
d93d7	Yanque, Renzo Lino - Peru
dd95ed	Demirtas, Gulnihal - Turkey
da205	Bagade, Abhijeet Dilip - India
db2c0	Hadi, Cherrak - France
db8a0	Cizmic, Milica - Serbia & Montenegro
dbcbd	Romero, Francisco - Mexico
dbcf7	Ickx, Wonne Hendrik - Belgium
dc154	Gudbrandsen O, Line - Norway
dc1d6	Figueroa Cardoza, Rudy Alexander - El Salvador
dc45b	Hila, Ben-avraham - Israel
dc655	Padilla, Victoria Maria - USA
dd1e0	Coshow, Drew Edward - USA
dd281	Ocampo, Nancy Elizabeth - Mexico
dd3f1	Tejada, Alberto Ricardo - Peru
dd45f	Yáñez, Diana Laura - Mexico
df376	Settimelli, Massimiliano - Italy
e05ff	Martinez, Daniel Marcelo - Argentina
e0fcc	Castillo, Tim Bryan - USA
e1c51	Lee, Sang Dae - South Korea
e1d8d	Juul, Gitte - Denmark
e1ec4	Gerard, Gutierrez Joy - Canada
e2dbq	Rusdi, Taufiq - Indonesia
e2edd	Barinov, Nikita Vladimirovich - Russia
e34a7	Seiler, Uwe Tobias - Germany
e3806	Ierace, Michele - Italy
e3ada	Brazil, James Peter - Australia
e506e	Pereira, Ricardo Nelson - Portugal
e5600	Arnabat, Jonathan - Spain
e59a6	Hey, Julia - Germany
e6a29	Pereyra, Nicolas Alejandro - Argentina
e6e80	Thompson, Daniel Caleb - USA
e7d36	Fifield, Jason - USA
e8130	Valente, Filipa Lima - Portugal
e824f	Dudas, Istvan - Hungary
e82db	minobe, Yukio - Japan
e8f23	Wastian, Ewald - Austria
e9a68	Raza, Syed Masood - Australia
e9ed2	Bench, David - USA
ea0cc	Riva, Diego - Argentina
ea1f9	Sauveplane, Alexandra Eugenie - France
ea385	Taboada, Cayetana - Argentina
ea9fa	Viramonte Moyano, Joaquin - Argentina
eafd2	Perrone, Simone - Italy
ebbcc	Wirz, Fulvio - Italy
ebd7a	Marion-landais, Jose Enrique - Dominican Republic
ebf57	Kayo, Otake - Japan
ec515	Rothfuss, Brigitte - Germany
ed411	Watson, Roger - USA

ee4eb	Witkowski, Boguslaw Franciszek - Belgium
eed99	Jander Janssen, Fabian - Chile
ef002	Drake, Tosh - USA
ef5f8	Zdravkovic, William Ilija - USA
efaf5	Förster, Tom - Germany
f060d	Pantoja, Rodrigo - Mexico
f0d7f	Bobadilla, Diana - Mexico
f0df5	Petrini, Valeria Soledad - Argentina
f13f3	Vaccari, Mirian Sayuri - Brazil
f1981	Olortegui, Ingrid Roxana - Peru
f1dcf	Nash, Joseph Colton - USA
f33a2	Ho, Jeong-der - Taiwan
f3538	Saul, Vega - USA
f448e	Leung, Stephen Siu-wye - Canada
f463d	Gutierrez, Hugo Velazquez - Mexico
f4a9b	Pattison, Julian Hunter - UK
f577d	Ahmed, Magda Badr - Egypt
f5947	Bhandari, Arun Ramesh - India
f6db7	Sil'nov, Alexander - Russia
f73ed	Purcell, Lee - USA
f7d82	Rizzello, Francesco - Italy
f844a	Castellano, Maria Jose - Argentina
f8504	Silva Lovera, Cristian Alejandro - Chile
f86eb	Kaminskij, Wladislaw Wladimirovicz - Belarus
f9008	Montanini, Laura - Italy
f977e	D'avezac De Castera, Loup Marie-Charles - France
f9e69	Saraiva, Susana Soares - Portugal
fac0e	L'hermite, Mélanie Nicole - France
fb959	Eremic Jocic, Sandra – Serbia & Montenegro
fba2f	Serrano Rodriguez, Pedro - Chile
fc3a2	Forte, Lucio - Italy
fc841	Marchisciana, Adriano Saverio - Italy
fcc8f	Maurice, Nicolas - France
fcced	Winiecki, Aaron Mathew - Australia
fda79	Shabander, Mohammed Sabah - Iraq
feb35	Yong, Martin Anthony - UK
feccb	Gustafson, Karl Andrew - USA
fee6a	Islam, Saiful - Bangladesh
ff5ad	Thomsen, Scott Christopher - USA
Xxxxx	Hugo N Lilli - Argentina

MY ENGLISH IS NOT SO GOOD, THEREFORE, YOU SHOULD TRANSLATE, SORRY!

Apreciados Sres de la F.A.A.C.
Sin deseos de premio ninguno, solo les envío algunas ideas para que las pongan en práctica si son factibles. Caso contrario, pueden arrojar esta carta al cesto de los papeles en desuso. Y disculpen la molestia que les ocasione el tiempo que les lleve leer ésto.

CASA AUTOSUSTENTABLE (ecologic-house)

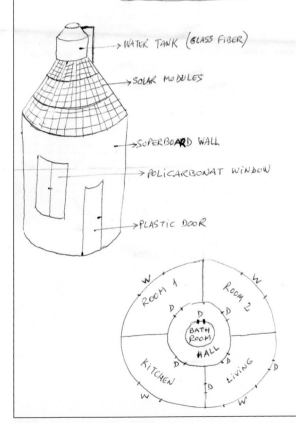

Letter from a world citizen

IaaC

Institut d'Arquitectura
Avançada de Catalunya
Pujades 102 baixos,
Poble Nou,
08005 Barcelona
Tel. 93 320 95 20
Fax 93 300 43 33
info@iaacat.com
www.iaacat.com

Director
Vicente Guallart

Development Director
Willy Müller

Project Manager
Lucas Cappelli

Comunication Director
Ramon Prat

Head of Finance
Salvador Estapé

Head of Studies
Carolien Ligtenberg

Communication Coordinator
Silvia Brandi

Secretary
M. Carme Guarch

Technical Support
Jesús Valdivia

Web Master
nitropix.com

Iaac
Institut
d'arquitectura
avançada
de Catalunya

1st Advanced Architecture Contest

Directors
Lucas Cappelli
Vicente Guallart

Coordinator
Luciana Asinari

Communication Events
Jorge Ledesma
Mateo Lima Valente

Contents Advisers
Jennifer Mack
Isabel Castro Olañeta
Gaston Jorge Gaye

Web Graphic Design
Leticia Peuser
Roxana Degiovanni
Franco Cappelli

Web Data Base
Emilio Degiovanni

Collaborators
Florise Pages
Nectarios Kefalogiannis
Silvia Brandi
Chris Kemper
Florence Yang
Jesus Lara

Jury Members
Vicente Guallart
Willy Müller
Manuel Gausa
Lucas Cappelli
Jose Luís Echevarría
Luis Falcón
François Roche
Jacob van Rijs
Marta Malé-Alemany
Aaron Betsky
José Miguel Iribas
Ramon Prat
Artur Serra
Salvador Rueda
Ignacio Jiménez de la Iglesia
J. M. Lin
Kim, Young Joon
Julio Gaeta
Felipe Pich-Aguilera
Marta Cervelló Casanova

www.advancedarchitecturecontest.org

Editors
IaaC. Institut d'Arquitectura Avançada de Catalunya
Actar

Responsibles of the edition
Vicente Guallart
Willy Müller
Lucas Cappelli

Coordination
Silvia Brandi

Classification texts
Leonardo Novelo

Translators
Meg Escudé
Cecilia Martin
Elaine Fradley

Collaborators
José Luis Echevarría
Maria Navas
Areti Markopoulo

Graphic design
Massimiliano Scaglione

Digital production
Oriol Rigat, Carmen Galán

Data recovery
Luciana Asinari

Production
Actar Pro

Printing
Ingoprint S.A.

Collaborators

Fundació UPC

ISBN 84-96540-43-X
D.L. B-29654-2006

Printed and bound in the European Union

Distribution
Actar D
Roca i Batlle 2
08023 Barcelona
tel +34 93 41 74 993
fax +34 93 41 86 707
office@actar-d.com
www.actar.es